CH

D0624874

AUG   2014

Westminster Public Library
3705 W. 112th Ave.
Westminster, CO 80031
www.westminsterlibrary.org

THE BASICS OF
BIOLOGY

CORE CONCEPTS

THE BASICS OF BIOLOGY

ANNE WANJIE, EDITOR

ROSEN
PUBLISHING®
New York

This edition published in 2014 by:

The Rosen Publishing Group, Inc.
29 East 21st Street
New York, NY 10010

Additional end matter copyright © 2014 by The Rosen Publishing Group, Inc.

All rights reserved. No part of this book may be reproduced in any form without permission in writing from the publisher, except by a reviewer.

Library of Congress Cataloging-in-Publication Data

Wanjie, Anne.
The basics of biology/Anne Wanjie.—1st ed.—New York: Rosen, © 2014
        p. cm.—(Core concepts)
Includes bibliographical references and index.
ISBN 978-1-4777-0554-4 (library binding)
1. Biology—Juvenile literature. I. Title.
QH309.2 .W36 2014
570

Manufactured in the United States of America

CPSIA Compliance Information: Batch #S13YA: For further information, contact Rosen Publishing, New York, New York, at 1-800-237-9932.

© 2004 Brown Bear Books Ltd.

CONTENTS

CHAPTER ONE

THE ESSENCE OF LIFE

Biology is the study of all aspects of living things great and small, from the chemicals that life forms are made of to where and how the life forms live. Scientists who specialize in biology are called biologists.

The history of biology begins more than 2,500 years ago, in the early civilizations of China, Europe, India, and the Middle East. In Western countries ancient Greek ideas about living creatures became the basis for the study of biology. Most of these ideas are now proven to be incorrect but were accepted for more than 2,000 years.

A marine biologist studies a coral reef off the coast of Fiji to determine the state of its health.

BLOOD AND PHLEGM

The ancient Greeks believed that everything on Earth was made of four elements: earth, air, fire, and water. The philosopher Hippocrates (460–377 BCE) suggested that people were made of these elements plus four fluids called humors. Two of these humors were blood (produced by the heart) and phlegm (from the brain). The other two were yellow bile (from the liver) and black bile (from the spleen). The levels of humors were thought to be responsible for a person's mental and physical health. This belief formed the basis of Western medicine for more than 2,000 years.

One question that ancient civilizations tried to answer was "What is the difference between living and nonliving things?" Some thought that the answer lay in different types of spirit or soul. Nonliving things had low-grade spirits. Plants had higher-grade spirits, animals had better-quality spirits than plants, and people had the highest grade of spirit.

In the 17th century many scientists began to doubt the old Greek ideas. They would no longer accept them just because they seemed to work. So, they developed new ideas backed up by the results of careful experiments. Their work laid the foundations of modern biology.

SPONTANEOUS GENERATION

A common belief in ancient times was that nonliving materials could create life. They did so by a mysterious process called spontaneous generation. When people saw hordes of flies coming from dead animals, they thought that the flesh had created the flies. They did not notice that the flies had hatched from eggs laid in the dead animal by female flies. For similar reasons they thought that frogs came from mud.

RECIPE FOR MICE

The chemist Johannes van Helmont (CE 1579–1644) made important discoveries about gases. But he also believed in spontaneous generation. He said that to make mice, you put dirty clothes in a barrel and add some wheat. After a few days the mixture of dirty clothes and wheat will produce mice.

THE TRUTH ABOUT FLIES

In 1668 the Italian physician Francisco Redi (1626–1697) disproved the old idea that rotting flesh created flies. He put one piece of meat into a flask with no lid. At the same time, he put another piece of meat into a flask and covered it with a lid. The lid kept flies from getting in. The meat in the open flask was soon seething with larvae, which turned into flies. But no maggots or flies emerged from the meat in the covered flask.

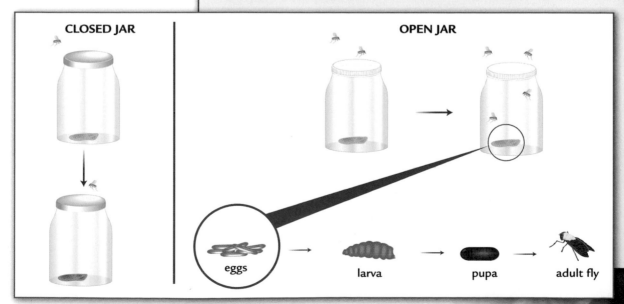

CLOSED JAR   OPEN JAR

eggs   larva   pupa   adult fly

VITALISM

An idea called vitalism took root in Europe in the early 17th century. According to this idea, living things had a "vital force" that gave them life. Nonliving things lacked this force. The chemicals that made up living things, or came from them, also carried some of this magical force—so it was impossible to make them artificially. The vitalism theory began to fall apart in 1828, when the German chemist Friedrich Wöhler (1800–1882) produced one of these chemicals in his laboratory. The substance he made, called urea, is a nitrogen-based substance present in urine.

The invention of the microscope in the mid-17th century was one of the biggest technical advances in biology. It allowed researchers to look at the structure of living things and see details invisible to the naked eye. By the end of the century scientists using microscopes had discovered plant and animal cells.

LIVING OR NOT LIVING?

Today biologists use a simple set of rules to decide if something is living or nonliving. For something to qualify as an organism (any type of living

Like animals and other living organisms, plants behave and respond to what happens around them. Stems grow upward and roots grow downward because the plant senses gravity. Leaves turn to face the light because the plant can sense the light's direction.

ARE VIRUSES LIFE FORMS?

The cells of all living organisms contain genetic (inherited) material in the form of RNA (ribonucleic acid) and DNA (deoxyribonucleic acid). Genetic material contains a complex chemical code. This code controls the growth, function, and reproduction of each cell and of the whole organism. Viruses are short strands of genetic material wrapped in a coat of protein. They invade the cells of organisms and mix the cells' genetic material with their own. They do this to reproduce, creating copies of themselves that go on to invade other cells. Although viruses contain genetic material and reproduce, most scientists do not class them as living organisms.

That is because they have no means of respiration or excretion. Viruses get all their energy from the cells that they invade.

thing), it must feed, respire, excrete, move, grow, reproduce, and sense its environment. Anything that carries out all seven of these functions is a living organism. If it does not perform all seven functions, it is not a living organism.

- **Feeding** is how an organism takes nutrients (food) from its surroundings.

- **Respiration** is the process that the organism uses to turn nutrients into energy. It uses this energy to power all the processes necessary for life, such as moving and growing.

- **Excretion** is the ways that an organism gets rid of the waste it creates when it produces and uses energy.

- **Movement** is used by all organisms from complex animals to simple single-celled bacteria to

DEFINITION OF LIFE
All living organisms:
- feed
- respire
- excrete
- move
- grow
- reproduce
- sense

Bacteria, like these *E. coli*, are simple organisms without complex behavior, but they grow, respire, excrete, reproduce, move, feed, and sense their surroundings.

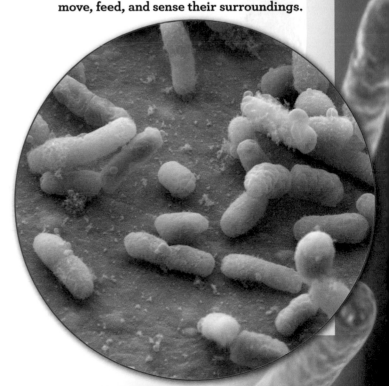

REPRODUCTION—A KEY TO LIFE

All life forms are able to reproduce themselves. There are two main ways of doing this, sexually and asexually. Many organisms reproduce asexually. It can be done by budding, in which one organism splits into two. Other creatures reproduce sexually. In this form of reproduction male sex cells (sperm) fuse with female sex cells (eggs) to form young. Young develop in many ways. They can grow inside the female or be laid as eggs or released as seeds in plants.

A bacterium divides into two through budding, or binary fission, a type of asexual reproduction.

find food, reproduce, escape danger, and find places to live. They may move by swimming, flying, walking, or sliding.

Pigs and other mammals reproduce sexually. Sperm from the male fertilizes the female's eggs. The young develop inside the female before they are born.

Birds also reproduce sexually. Their young develop inside an egg that the female lays in a nest.

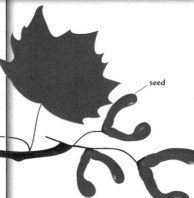

seed

Many plants also reproduce sexually. The fertilized eggs develop into seeds. Some, such as sycamore seeds, drift on the wind to new areas.

Most plants do not move from one place to another, but they do move toward light and away from the direction of gravity. They push their roots down into the soil to find minerals and water.

- **Growing** plants usually keep growing throughout their lives, but most animals stop growing when they reach a certain size.

- **Reproduction** is the process of creating offspring. Most microorganisms reproduce by splitting into two identical parts. Plants reproduce by making seeds that grow into new plants or by budding. Animals lay eggs or give birth to live young.

- **Sensitivity** is an organism's ability to react to things happening around it. Microorganisms react to chemicals that lead them to their food. They also react to changes in temperature and moisture levels, so they can find suitable places to live.

Most plants do not respond rapidly to their surroundings. Some can react quickly, however; the sensitive plant, or mimosa, shows this clearly. It reacts to being touched by curling up its leaves. The plant does this by drawing water from structural cells inside its leaves.

The sensitivity of plants includes their response to changes in light. Plants turn to face the light or open their flowers during the day and close them again as night falls.

Animals use their senses, such as sight, touch, smell, and hearing, to gather information about their surroundings. That helps them move, find food, and reproduce.

HOW LIFE IS ORGANIZED

Biology is not just about the study of organisms. It also includes how organisms relate to each other and to the environment they live in. To understand these relationships, biologists study the different levels of life organization. These levels build up to form a complete picture of the organism and how it fits in with its surroundings.

The lowest level of biological organization is a molecule. A molecule is made of two or more atoms. Atoms are the smallest possible parts of chemical elements, such as carbon or oxygen. Molecules contain different combinations and numbers of atoms.

In a living organism molecules range in size from those with just a few atoms to huge, complicated molecules called macromolecules. Macromolecules include the common building blocks of an organism: fats, carbohydrates, such as starch, and millions of types of proteins. Macromolecules combine to form the

BACK TO LIFE

Dried yeast looks like a lifeless, pale-brown powder, but you can bring it to life with water and sugar. Put around 1 inch (2.5cm) of warm water (cooler than 100°F, 38°C) into a clean plastic bottle, such as a soda bottle. Add half a teaspoon of dried yeast from a grocery store. Swirl the bottle for a few seconds to mix the yeast and water. Now add a teaspoon of sugar, and swirl the bottle again. The dried yeast will come to life, feed on the sugar, and give off carbon dioxide gas. Fit the neck of a balloon over the top of the bottle. What do you see happening? Why do you think it happens?

ASTROBIOLOGY

Biologists studying the possibility of life on other planets are called astrobiologists. Studying bacteria that live in extreme conditions on Earth helps astrobiologists figure out how life might exist on other planets. These extreme conditions include lakes beneath the ice of Antarctica and the waters around underwater volcanoes.

LEVELS OF ORGANIZATION

The living world can be divided into larger and larger levels of organization, from atoms and molecules to cells, to organisms and ecosystems, and finally the biosphere.

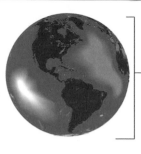

13. BIOSPHERE
The biomes of the world make up the zone of life on Earth called the biosphere.

12. BIOME
Regions such as rivers (below) or deserts are classified into biomes.

10. HABITAT
A habitat is a type of area, such as this reed bed, in which certain communities occur.

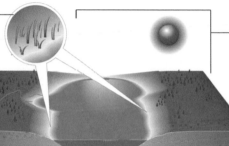

11. ECOSYSTEM
Habitats, communities, and nonliving parts of the environment (soil, water, and sunlight) form an ecosystem.

9. COMMUNITY
Populations of different species living in the same area form a community.

8. POPULATION
Individual organisms of the same type (species) living in the same area form a population.

7. ORGANISM
Body systems combine in an organism.

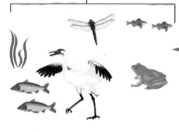

6. SYSTEM
Organs form body systems, such as the digestive system.

5. ORGAN
Tissues form organs such as the stomach.

1. ATOM
The smallest possible part of an element that can exist.

2. MOLECULE
Groups of atoms form molecules.

3. CELL
Molecules such as proteins and sugars form tiny cells, the building blocks of all life.

4. TISSUE
Cells form tissues.

walls and insides of cells, which are the smallest units of life. Proteins also carry out and control the chemical processes that enable cells to function.

All bacteria, some fungi, and many algae are single cells. Larger organisms such as plants and animals are multicellular. They consist of billions of cells of different types. In these organisms cells form tissues such as bone and muscle. Tissues form organs such as hearts, lungs, and flowers. Organs form systems, including the digestive system and nervous system. Several interacting

A Cape fur seal is shaped for its underwater habitat. It can only move slowly when it returns to land to rest and breed.

OUTER SPACE MOLECULES

Most scientists believe that life on Earth began when chemicals in prehistoric oceans combined to form ever-more-complex molecules. These molecules eventually became the first, simple forms of life. They formed simple cells, which then combined over millions of years to create larger organisms. Some scientists, however, think that the first complex molecules were formed out in space and that comets carried them to Earth.

LIFE ON OTHER WORLDS

The only life we know about is here on Earth, but there is no reason to believe that there is no life on other worlds. Life might have developed on planets orbiting distant stars. There might even be life on planets and moons in our own solar system.

In 1996 scientists claimed they had found evidence of life on Mars. This lay inside a meteorite found in Antarctica. The meteorite was a small rock formed around 4 billion years ago on Mars.

It was blasted away from the surface by the impact of an asteroid. The rock traveled through space before landing on Earth around 13,000 years ago. The meteorite contained strange, microscopic imprints and traces of chemicals that usually come from living organisms. Scientists thought that the imprints and chemicals had been made by tiny Martian microorganisms. But other scientists disagreed and suggested other causes of these possible signs of life. For example, the meteorite contains traces of substances called carbonates, which could possibly have come from bacteria. But carbonates are also common in nonliving materials.

systems form the whole organism.

At a higher level of organization all the populations of organisms living in a region function as an ecosystem. An ecosystem is an interacting, interconnected web of life forms and their environment. In an ecosystem the different organisms live, feed, breed, and die in a continuous cycle. Plants live by taking nutrients from the soil and using sunlight to create food. Animals eat the plants and one another. When animals and plants die, bacteria and chemical reactions break down their bodies, and the nutrients they contain go back into the soil and continue the cycle.

Every organism in an ecosystem is adapted to the type of place, or habitat, it lives in. Adaptation is how evolution occurs. Over several generations a group of organisms changes and becomes better able to survive.

In adapting to different habitats, organisms often have to trade one advantage for another. In seals and sea lions, for example, flippers evolved from legs. The flippers make these animals good swimmers, adapted for catching the fish they feed on. But having flippers instead of legs makes them slow and clumsy when they are on land.

? If there was life on other planets, would it be the same as or different than life on Earth? If there were alien life forms, how would we recognize them as living?

MANUFACTURED LIFE FORMS

In 1999 scientists made a breakthrough that may lead to the creation of artificial life forms. The scientists found that although a bacteria called *Mycoplasma genitalium* has around 480 genes (segments of inherited material), only 300 are essential for life.

In theory artificial bacteria could be created by replacing the nonessential genes with humanmade versions. The new bacteria will be able to survive and reproduce. Artificial bacteria may be created to clean up pollution, for example, but this research is highly controversial.

NAMING AND CLASSIFYING SPECIES

Early naturalists could see that some life forms were similar and others were not. But until Linnaeus devised his system for naming and classifying life forms, there was no logical system to arrange them. Linnaeus introduced the use of two-part names for every species and put each species in a series of ever larger groups called a hierarchy.

Every species has a two-part name in Latin. The first part is a genus name shared with closely related species. The second part, the specific name, refers to just one species. The scientific name of the leopard is *Panthera pardus*. *Panthera* is the name of the genus that includes most of the big cats, while *pardus* specifies the leopard alone.

The bobcat *(Felis rufa; right)* belongs to the genus *Felis*. Other members of the genus *Felis* include lynxes and wildcats.

The domestic cat *(Felis domesticus; left)* has the same genus name as the bobcat but a different specific name, *domesticus*.

organelles performs an important task for the cell.

Bacteria are classed in a separate domain, Prokaryota. A prokaryote cell contains neither a membrane-enclosed nucleus nor organelles.

FROM PHYLUM TO SPECIES

Related species are grouped into a genus (plural genera). Closely related genera are further grouped into families. For example, all cats belong to one family,

Scientists once placed the cougar in the same genus as bobcats and domestic tabbies and called it *Felis concolor*. It is much larger, however, and is now classified in a different genus called *Puma*.

HOW TO DEFINE A SPECIES

In 1942 biologist Ernst Mayr (1904–2005) suggested that species are populations of organisms whose individuals can breed with each other. So, a lion can breed with other lions but cannot breed with a leopard or any other animal. This explains why species remain separate and clearly defined.

However, this concept does not include species that do not reproduce sexually, that is, by exchanging genes . Bacteria, for example, only sometimes exchange genes. Also, different species do sometimes breed to create hybrids. Wheat, for example, is a hybrid of two different species of plants.

the Felidae. Families are placed together into orders, such as the Carnivora, which includes the cat family, as well as all other mammals, such as dogs, that have four sharp cheek teeth (the word *carnivore* refers to all meat-eating animals, but not all are within the order Carnivora.) Orders are then grouped into classes, such as

the Mammalia, or mammals. Classes of plants are grouped into divisions, while classes of animals are grouped into phyla (singular phylum). Each of the phyla includes organisms that share certain features. Phylum Arthropoda, for example, includes at least 1 million species of invertebrates (animals that do not have a backbone), including spiders, insects, and crabs. Although they may look very different, all arthropods have a hard outer covering, or exoskeleton, and jointed appendages that form legs, mouthparts, and antennae.

THE END OF CLASSES?

Because animals descend from a common ancestor, some biologists think we should throw out the old classification system altogether. Instead, we should organize species on an entirely cladistic basis. This means species would not be placed in a hierarchy of classes but simply identified by a clade or branch depending on a common inherited trait. All animals born from shelled eggs, for instance, would be assigned to the same clade. Other biologists think this system would be impractical because organisms would no longer be placed in convenient pigeonholes.

SUPERCLASSES AND SUBORDERS

Not all organisms fit neatly into the order–class–phylum system. For many animal groups, such as insects and snakes, intermediate levels such as superclasses and suborders are created. New discoveries force biologists to rethink classifications, adding new levels or moving a species to a different group. Even the established system that follows the hierarchy of small groups within larger groups may be changed. Some scientists think that a hierarchy is not the best way to describe the natural world around us and want to rebuild the whole classification system anew.

DEFINING A SPECIES

A species is generally defined as a group of organisms that can breed with each other. The word *species* comes from a Latin term meaning "appearance," and biologists originally identified species by the way they looked.

A species was simply a group of animals that looked the same. Looking at an organism's shape and form, or

NAMING AND CLASSIFYING SPECIES

In 1950 Willi Hennig (1913–1976), a German insect specialist, introduced the idea of cladistics. The word *cladistics* comes from a Greek word meaning "branch," and cladistics involves the construction of branching networks that trace the ancestry of a species.

Cladistics compares large numbers of characteristics among species to build up a family tree for a range of species. This tree is called a cladogram. Cladograms show points in the evolution of the group when certain key characteristics emerged for the first time. Within a cladogram there are sets of branches called clades. Each clade begins with one common ancestor, then branches out into all of its descendants, which share the same key feature or features. A branch showing leopards, domestic cats, and all their relatives descending from a common ancestor would form a clade. A group of branches showing that carnivores such as

MAKING A CLADOGRAM

Once you have the right information, cladograms are simple to construct. Try completing the cladogram on the right yourself. The list here shows features possessed by lions, salamanders, tortoises, lampreys, and tuna. Decide where these animals should appear on the cladogram (circles 1–5) based on which features each animal has.

1. **Backbone:** Lions, tortoises, salamanders, tuna, and lampreys have one.

2. **Jaws:** Lions, tortoises, salamanders, and tunas have them; lampreys do not.

3. **Four walking legs:** Lions, tortoises, and salamanders have them; lampreys and tuna do not have legs.

4. **Waterproof skin:** Tortoises and lions have one; the rest do not.

5. **Hair:** Lions have hair, but none of the other creatures do.

cats, dogs, and bears descend from a common ancestor is another.

Unlike biologists making traditional family trees, biologists using cladistics do not look for "shared primitive characters," which are common traits that date back long before the group being studied developed. One such character is a mammal's backbone, a feature that also occurs in animals such as fish and reptiles. Instead, cladistics focuses on when a new feature that defines the group first appeared. This feature is called a "shared derived character." In mammals hair is a shared derived character. So, a biologist constructing a cladogram figures out the point at which hair first appeared and starts the mammal clade from there.

Cladistics is important because it helps reduce confusion caused by convergent evolution. The evolutionary history of species is called phylogeny.

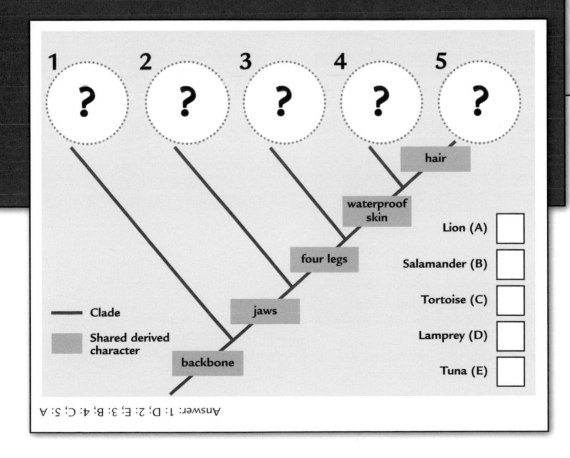

Legend:
- Clade
- Shared derived character

Shared derived characters (bottom to top): backbone, jaws, four legs, waterproof skin, hair

Species: Lion (A), Salamander (B), Tortoise (C), Lamprey (D), Tuna (E)

Answer: 1: D; 2: E; 3: B; 4: C; 5: A

CONVERGENT EVOLUTION

American woodchucks look similar to Australian wombats. They are both small, sharp-toothed, furry burrowing creatures that graze on grasses, roots, and tubers. The resemblance might lead you to think they are related. The wombat in fact belongs to an entirely different order of animals, the marsupials, or pouched mammals. The likeness is a result of convergent evolution, which happens when two unrelated species evolve similar features in response to a similar environment.

WHAT IS A SUBSPECIES?

Over a species' range populations from different areas may vary in features such as size, color, and shape. However, individuals from different populations can still breed together. Biologists call these separate populations subspecies. For example, male red-winged blackbirds that live in the eastern U.S. have a yellow patch on their wings, while those in parts of California have an orange patch. Each forms a separate subspecies.

Biologists add an extra part to the end of a scientific name to signify a subspecies. For example, California red-winged blackbirds are called *Agelaius phoeniceus californicus*.

plains zebras living in different parts of Africa. They differ in appearance but do not form separate species because the different populations can interbreed. Populations like these are called subspecies.

Other animals look similar because they have evolved to suit similar habitats. This is called convergent evolution.

THE DIVERSITY OF SPECIES

Life on Earth is astonishingly diverse, with up to several millions of different species in the oceans, in the soil, and on land. According to the World Wildlife Fund's Living Planet Index, there are about 300,000 plant species, 4,000 species of mammals, 6,300 reptile species, 4,200 species of amphibians, 19,100 fish species, more than 1 million insect species, and about 400,000 other invertebrates, including roughly 35,000 spiders. These are merely the numbers of species known to science. Biologists think the actual number of species may be more than 5 million, while some estimates are as high as 100 million species!

morphology, is still the easiest way to identify many species. You can tell a red fox from other kinds of dogs by its bushy tail, for example.

Appearances can be deceptive, however. There are several populations of

FUNGI

Mushrooms, toadstools, yeasts, mildews, and the molds that grow on bread all belong to a group of organisms called fungi.

Fungi form their own separate kingdom, containing at least 70,000 different species. They are not plants, and they have no chlorophyll (the green pigment that absorbs energy from sunlight). Genetic tests suggest they are more closely related to animals than to plants, but fungi are not animals either.

Because they cannot make their own food as plants do, fungi eat plants and animals. Parasitic fungi feed on living organisms. Saprophytic fungi feed on plant and animal remains. Both types eat by releasing chemicals called enzymes that digest what the fungi are feeding on. The fungi absorb nutrients and minerals from their food. Chemicals released by some mold fungi give blue cheese its flavor.

Fungi are made of numerous cottonlike threads called hyphae, which absorb nutrients. Hyphae spread out in a tangled mass through the soil in ground-based fungi or within the tissues of the plant or animal host. The mass of hyphae is called a mycelium. Sometimes hyphae can clump together to form fruiting bodies such as toadstools, or they form pinheads, such as the mold on rotting fruit.

The fruiting body is often the only visible part of a fungus. It is the part that distributes spores, which are the fungal equivalent of pollen and seeds. Small fruiting bodies cover these cheeses, but most of the fungus body is a mesh of hyphae running throughout the cheese.

These shapes, called stromatolites, are among the most ancient of fossils. They formed billions of years ago when mats of bacteria became covered by mud. All of Earth's diverse life forms evolved from bacterialike microorganisms.

When life on Earth began, there were just bacterialike organisms. All the countless species that have lived in the past and are alive now have gradually evolved from these life forms.

THE EMERGENCE OF NEW SPECIES

New species emerge when one species splits into two or more populations. The groups may be separated by physical barriers, such as oceans, mountain ranges, or rivers, or by their behavior—perhaps one group is active at dawn and the other at dusk. If the groups are separated for long enough, natural variations between the populations eventually lead to their being unable to interbreed. A new species has thus formed. This is called speciation.

HOW MANY SPECIES?

Experts have estimated there are about 1.7 million species in the world. But these estimates are based on limited information. There are two to three times as many tropical birds as temperate birds. Yet most of the 1.4 million insects and other invertebrates identified are from the temperate region. If there turn out to be as many more of these small creatures in the tropics as there are birds, then their total number could be many more than 5 million. After taking samples in Panama, one researcher estimated there may be as many as 30 million insect species on Earth. Estimates that include species of microorganisms reach as high as 100 million species.

TARGETING HOT SPOTS

In recent years some biologists have focused on the idea of biodiversity hot spots. They are small areas of the world where a huge number of species are concentrated, such as Madagascar, Costa Rica, and the Philippines.

Research by environmental scientists suggests that nearly half of all plant species and more than a third of all land-living vertebrates (animals with backbones) live in just 25 small areas of the world. Some conservationists argue that if this is so, people should not worry about biodiversity everywhere. Instead, we should focus on preserving hot spots at all costs from destruction by human activity.

Many hot-spot species, such as this ring-tailed lemur from Madagascar, are endemic—they live nowhere else.

AT-RISK SPECIES

In recent years the number of species, or biodiversity, has suddenly taken a dramatic downturn due to the activities of people. Today there are more than 5,000 species in the "at risk" category, and many more are under threat. Even optimistic estimates suggest a quarter of all mammal and amphibian species, 11 percent of birds, 20 percent of reptiles, and 34 percent of fish are in danger of extinction by the year 2020. There may also be a loss of up to 47 percent of all known plant types—a total of at least 144,000 species.

DO WE NEED BIODIVERSITY?

Some people cannot see any need for preserving biodiversity. If a species is no longer able to survive, they argue, it is natural that it should die out. Conservationists, however, argue that loss of diversity reduces the gene pool (the total variety of inherited traits). A wide gene pool allows new species to evolve if disaster strikes the dominant species. Biologists think the same dangers apply to our food crops and animals, which come from just a handful of species. If any one of them were lost to disease, the loss to our food supply could be catastrophic.

EVOLUTIONARY EMBRYOS?

Looking at similarities between animals can be misleading. In 1866 German zoologist Ernst Haeckel (1834–1919) proposed that an organism's development reflects its evolutionary history. Haeckel suggested that a human embryo goes through stages similar to a microorganism and later develops gill slits like a fish.

Later biologists completely disproved Haeckel's theory. They showed that embryos never pass through stages in which structures of adult ancestors are present. It was also discovered that the diagrams of embryos that Haeckel used to justify his work were faked. The tissues that Haeckel believed were gill slits are never used for breathing. In fish they develop into true gills, but in people they develop into bones of the jaw and inner ear.

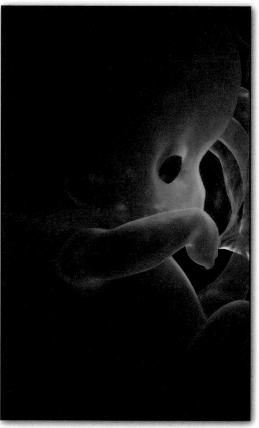
Human embryo in the uterus.

FAMILY TREES

The grouping of species into different levels is not just a valuable sorting task. It also provides information about the relationships that different species share. Since Charles Darwin (1809–1882) published his theory of natural selection in 1859, it has become clear that the groupings depend on the idea that every species is descended from a common ancestor. All mammals, for instance, descend from a single mammal species that appeared about 220 million years ago. The descendants of this animal include the first mammals with sharp cheek teeth for shearing meat.

In turn, their descendants divided into species, and the order Carnivora emerged.

Among the early carnivores was a cat-like animal whose descendants formed the cat family. Again, among the first cat's descendants was a cat that evolved into the genus *Panthera*, which includes lions, leopards, and other big cats of today.

By classifying animals and plants, scientists not only sort them into categories but also construct a kind of family tree of animal and plant species.

SHARED CHARACTERISTICS

The presence of shared characteristics is called homology. Biologists look, for instance, for likenesses in organisms' anatomies (the shape and structure of the body). Human arms, the front legs of a cat, whale flippers, and bat wings look very different. But under the skin the bones are remarkably similar. The basic mammalian bone structure has been altered by evolution to suit each species' lifestyle, whether climbing, running, swimming, or flying.

MOLECULAR LIKENESSES

Biologists have looked at the likenesses of organisms right down to the level of their molecules, such as proteins and DNA, using advanced laboratory techniques. They have revealed that related organisms share similar proteins. The proteins of unrelated life forms show greater differences. Hemoglobin is one protein that scientists use to trace how closely animal species are related. It is a protein in the blood that carries oxygen around the body. Amino acids are small molecules that build proteins by forming chains and sheets. Hemoglobin is made of a chain of about 146 amino acids. Gorilla hemoglobin differs from human hemoglobin by just one amino acid, showing that gorillas are closely related to us. Mice have 27 different amino acids in their hemoglobin, so they are more distantly related.

Gorillas and humans share around 98 percent of their genetic makeup.

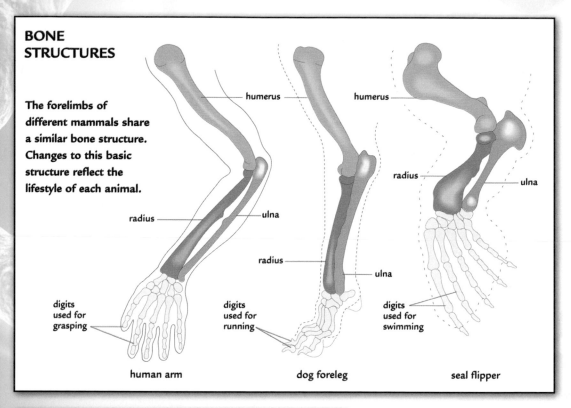

BONE STRUCTURES

The forelimbs of different mammals share a similar bone structure. Changes to this basic structure reflect the lifestyle of each animal.

humerus

humerus

radius — ulna

radius

ulna

radius

ulna

digits used for grasping

digits used for running

digits used for swimming

human arm

dog foreleg

seal flipper

SEAL OF APPROVAL

Walruses, seals, and sea lions have long been grouped together in the order Pinnipedia. A closer study of their anatomy has recently revealed some unexpected differences. In fact, the anatomical differences are enough to suggest they may have evolved from two or more unrelated carnivores. If this is proven correct, these animals should be grouped in separate orders.

Information from new techniques, such as looking at organisms' genes, is making many biologists reassess traditional approaches to classification. New World vultures look very similar to those from Africa and Asia. In the 1990s, however, scientists used a technique called DNA hybridization to compare their genes. This showed that New World vultures are in fact more closely related to storks.

Sometimes, a feature loses its function, evolves to be smaller, and is eventually lost altogether. Features like these are called vestigial, and they can give important clues to a species' ancestry. Boa snakes, for example, have tiny vestigial legs complete with a little claw inherited from their walking ancestors.

Like other animals, people have vestigial organs, too. The appendix is part of the gut that may become infected and need to be removed. It serves no function in humans but is important

GENETIC SPECIES MARKERS

One new way of testing whether a plant or animal is a separate species is to look at the DNA molecules, or genes, in its cells to see if the organism contains its own unique genetic identity. DNA is the chemical code that carries the organism's complete instructions for life and its entire inheritance since genes are passed down from one generation to the next.

The DNA molecule is a long chain of small molecules called nucleotides. There are four types, abbreviated A, C, T, and G. The sequence of nucleotides provides the instructions to the cell. By comparing the sequences of As, Cs, Ts, and Gs in different species, biologists can spot similarities and differences. Differences in the sequences point to differences in ancestry; similarities can prove that species are closely related. This technique has allowed the discovery of some new species. The African forest elephant, for instance, was thought to be a subspecies of the African elephant. Genetic testing has shown that the forest elephant is an entirely separate species.

for plant-eating mammals—it helps them digest their food. This suggests that humans are distantly descended from plant-eating mammals.

Not all likenesses are homologies. Other likenesses, called analogies, occur when unrelated species develop similar features in response to similar environments. Bats and birds both have wings, for example. The wings look similar, but the bones supporting them are completely different. This shows that these groups developed both wings and the power of flight independently.

CHAPTER THREE

LIFE AT THE MOLECULAR LEVEL

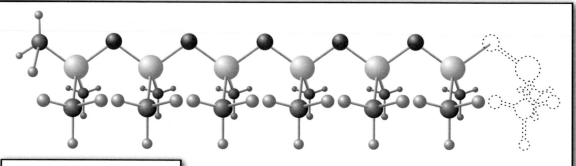

- Carbon atom
- Oxygen atom
- Hydrogen atom
- Silicon atom

Molecule:
This compound is made of thousands of molecules.

Atoms combine to form molecules. Molecules sometimes link together to form long chains. This molecule is called polydimethylsiloxane.

All living things on the planet are made up of tiny carbon-containing particles that include proteins, carbohydrates, and lipids.

Everything on Earth, both living and nonliving, is made up of chemical elements (substances with one type of atom). The atoms of these elements combine to make molecules, and in turn the molecules combine to form matter—the solids, liquids, and gases that make up ourselves and the world around us. Some molecules consist of atoms of a single element. Other molecules, called compounds, contain atoms of two or more elements. The study of the chemistry of life is biochemistry, and the molecules of living things are called biochemical molecules. In living organisms the most important biochemical molecules are carbohydrates, lipids, proteins, and nucleic acids such as DNA. Biochemists who study biochemical molecules are called molecular biologists.

KEKULE'S SNAKE

By the middle of the 19th century scientists had figured out how carbon atoms form long chains. However, the structure of some common carbon-based molecules puzzled them. One of these molecules was benzene. Scientists knew that it had six carbon atoms and six hydrogen atoms, but they could not figure out how they were linked together. In 1865 the German chemist Friedrich August Kekule von Stradonitz (1829–1896) fell asleep while working on this problem. He dreamed that a snake bit its own tail. The dream gave him the idea, which proved to be true, that the carbon atoms in benzene might be arranged in a ring. The discovery that carbon atoms could form rings was one of the most important advances in organic chemistry. It enabled scientists to understand the structures of a wide range of molecules based on rings of carbon and other atoms. These molecules include sugars, starches, amino acids, and proteins.

benzene molecule

ELEMENTAL LIFE

There are 92 naturally occurring elements on Earth. Living things are made up of fewer than 20 of these elements, although organisms use many more to keep their internal systems working. The most important elements are carbon, hydrogen, oxygen, and nitrogen. These four elements make up more than 95 percent of the weight of all the living organisms on Earth.

CARBON COMPOUNDS

The key element in biochemical molecules is carbon. Atoms of carbon

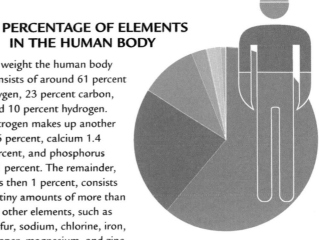

PERCENTAGE OF ELEMENTS IN THE HUMAN BODY

By weight the human body consists of around 61 percent oxygen, 23 percent carbon, and 10 percent hydrogen. Nitrogen makes up another 2.6 percent, calcium 1.4 percent, and phosphorus 1.1 percent. The remainder, less then 1 percent, consists of tiny amounts of more than 50 other elements, such as sulfur, sodium, chlorine, iron, copper, magnesium, and zinc.

61 %	Oxygen	1.4 %	Calcium
23 %	Carbon	1.1 %	Phosphorus
10 %	Hydrogen	0.9 %	Other elements, including sulfur, sodium, chlorine, iron, copper, magnesium, and zinc.
2.6 %	Nitrogen		

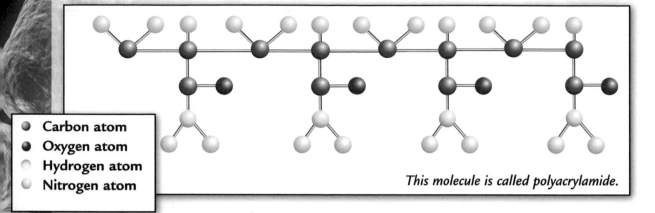

- ● Carbon atom
- ● Oxygen atom
- ○ Hydrogen atom
- ○ Nitrogen atom

This molecule is called polyacrylamide.

combine easily with one another and the atoms of other elements. They also link together to form long chains called polymers, with atoms of other elements attached. These chains can be straight, forked, or joined up as rings. They form the basis for the very large molecules that make up living things.

Carbon compounds are called organic compounds because in the 19th century most of the known carbon compounds came from living organisms.

SILICON LIFE

All life forms on Earth are based on carbon. Biologists debate whether that would be the same on other planets. One idea about alien life forms is that they could be based on silicon instead of carbon because silicon bonds with the atoms of other elements in a way similar to carbon. Many scientists think silicon-based life is unlikely because silicon cannot form the very large, stable molecules present in living things. Some molecules contain tens of thousands of carbon atoms, but the largest natural silicon molecule contains only six silicon atoms.

Glucose is a type of carbohydrate called a monosaccharide. There are six carbon atoms in each molecule. Five carbon atoms are joined in a ring, with hydrogen and oxygen atoms attached. The chemical formula of glucose is $C_6H_{12}O_6$.

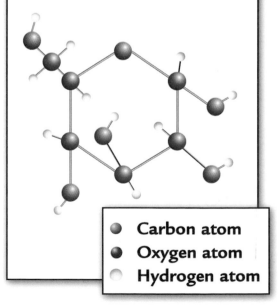

- ● Carbon atom
- ● Oxygen atom
- ○ Hydrogen atom

Scientists have now identified more than a million different carbon compounds. Some of them come from living organisms; but many others, such as industrial chemicals and plastics, are synthetically made (artificial). Compounds that do not contain carbon (for example, water) are called inorganic compounds.

CARBO ENERGY

Carbohydrates are important biochemical molecules for humans because they provide most of the body's energy. The simplest carbohydrates are sugars called monosaccharides. A molecule of a monosacchride has a central ring made of atoms of carbon and oxygen. This ring has carbon, hydrogen, and oxygen atoms attached to it. Fructose, glucose, and galactose are examples of typical monosaccharides. Glucose is used as fuel by animal and plant cells; it is burned to produce energy.

Monosaccharide molecules can join together in twos (making sugars called disaccharides) and in long chains to form polysaccharides. Examples of polysaccharides are cellulose, glycogen, and starch. Cellulose molecules are straight chains of glucose molecules. Cellulose is the main ingredient of the cell walls of plants. Glycogen molecules are long glucose chains with many side branches. Animals store glycogen in their livers and convert it into glucose when they need energy. Blood carries the glucose to the muscles and organs that need it. Starch is similar to glycogen, but its molecules have fewer branches. Plants store starch and change it into glucose to provide energy.

INSULIN INJECTIONS

In the human body an organ called the pancreas produces the hormone insulin. Insulin helps control the levels of glucose in the bloodstream. If glucose levels get too high, the insulin tells the liver to change the glucose into glycogen and store it until it is needed. People with a medical condition called diabetes do not produce enough insulin, and so their blood glucose levels can get too high. This problem can make them very ill. Some people with diabetes need to inject themselves with insulin to help control their blood glucose levels.

STEROIDS

Steroids are lipids based on four linked rings of carbon atoms. They occur in some types of hormones and vitamins. Anabolic steroids are synthetic hormones that help people gain weight after long illnesses because they boost the production of muscle-building proteins. Some athletes and bodybuilders take anabolic steroids illegally to build up muscles. Misuse of steroids can cause serious problems, such as liver damage and increased aggression.

OILS, FATS, AND WAXES

Oils, fats, and waxes are all lipids. Fats store energy and protect organs with padding, while oils and waxes protect the skin and hair. Most lipids are made of glycerol or glycerine and fatty acids. Glycerol is a natural alcohol made up of carbon, hydrogen, and oxygen. A fatty acid is a chain of carbon atoms with hydrogen atoms attached to them.

The most common fats we have are lipids called triglycerides. A triglyceride is one molecule of glycerol attached to three molecules of fatty acids. The body stores triglycerides in fat cells. Turning glycerol into glucose produces energy.

THE BUILDING BLOCKS OF LIFE

Proteins are the basic structural materials of all plant and animal cells. They control and carry out the chemical processes that enable cells to function. Proteins are called the building blocks of life because they are so important. Protein molecules contain carbon, hydrogen, oxygen, and nitrogen. Many proteins also contain sulfur, iron, and phosphorus.

The cells of all living organisms make proteins from amino acids. Amino acids are based on carbon, hydrogen, nitrogen, and oxygen. Twenty different types of amino acids occur in living creatures. Cells join them into long chains of amino acid molecules to form substances called polypeptides. Then the cells shape the polypeptides into protein molecules.

The two main groups of proteins are fibrous proteins and globular proteins. The polypeptides in fibrous proteins are either twisted or coiled. They help make tough body tissues such as muscle cells and fingernails. In globular proteins the polypeptides are folded in compact, rounded shapes. Important globular

MAKING PROTEIN GLUE

Milk contains a protein called casein. You can separate the casein from milk and make it into glue.

1. Put half a cup of milk into a small bowl, and stir in 2 tablespoons of vinegar. Keep stirring the mixture until no more lumps form.

2. Line a kitchen strainer with a paper towel. Hold the strainer over a bowl, and pour the mixture into it. The paper towel will catch the lumps in the mixture. Gently blot the lumps with more paper towels to squeeze out all the liquid.

3. Rinse out the first bowl, and then scrape the lumps into it. Stir in 2 tablespoons of water and half a teaspoon of baking soda. Keep stirring and adding small amounts of baking powder until no more bubbles appear. You have made casein glue.

GLOBULAR OR FIBROUS?

All proteins are made of chains of amino acids:

amino acids — protein chain (polypeptide)

Most proteins are either globular or fibrous:

Fibrous proteins are made up of twisted or coiled polypeptides.

polypeptides

collagen (a fibrous protein)

Globular proteins are made up of folded polypeptides.

polypeptides

hemoglobin (a globular protein)

Examples of globular proteins

cell
hormone
cell wall

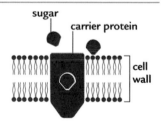

sugar
carrier protein
cell wall

1. Hormones are released by cells to send messages.

2. Carrier proteins transport sugars and amino acids.

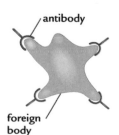

antibody
foreign body

3. Antibodies attack foreign proteins.

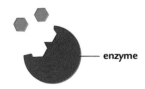

enzyme

4. Enzymes act as catalysts to speed up chemical reactions.

proteins include some hormones (such as insulin), carrier proteins, antibodies, and enzymes.

Hormones act as chemical messengers, helping control the function of organs and other systems. Carrier proteins take important molecules around the body. Hemoglobin, for example, carries oxygen in the blood. Antibodies form part of an animal's defense against infection. They attack foreign proteins (called antigens) that enter the body.

ENZYME CATALYSTS

Enzymes are proteins that drive biochemical reactions. They act as catalysts, which are substances that enable reactions to take place, usually at a faster rate, but emerge from them unchanged. Each type of enzyme speeds up a single type of chemical reaction.

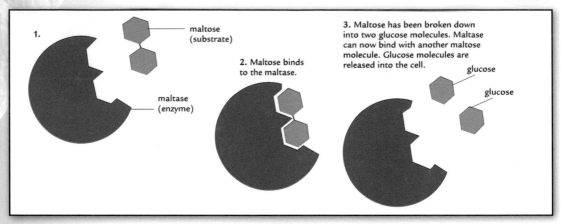

The molecule that an enzyme acts on is called the substrate. Substrate molecules fit perfectly into cavities on a particular enzyme. After the reaction the unchanged enzyme can be used again in another reaction. Here, the enzyme maltase breaks a molecule of the sugar maltose into two molecules of glucose.

ENZYMES

In 1926 U.S. biochemist James Batcheller Sumner (1887–1955) became the first person to produce a purified enzyme called urease, which breaks down urea. He also proved that urease and most other enzymes are types of proteins. His work on enzymes and proteins earned him a share of the 1946 Nobel Prize for chemistry.

The names of enzymes are often formed by combining the name of the substance they work on and the ending "ase." For example, glucase is the enzyme that breaks down glucose, lipases break down lipids, and proteases break down proteins.

In an enzyme the polypeptides are folded to create a cavity with a precise shape. The molecule an enzyme works on is called the substrate. The substrate fits exactly into the cavity of the enzyme, like a key fitting into a lock. The reaction begins as soon as the substrate is in place.

Some enzymes break the substrate down into two or more smaller products in a reaction called a catabolic reaction. Other enzymes combine two or more substrates to create a larger product. This reaction is called an anabolic reaction.

Plants and animals use catabolic reactions to convert complex molecules into simpler substances. That is what happens in cellular respiration, when enzymes break down food to release energy. Organisms use anabolic reactions to create complex molecules from simpler ones, such as making starch from glucose and proteins from amino acids.

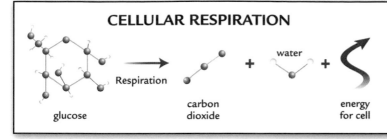

CELLULAR RESPIRATION

glucose → Respiration → carbon dioxide + water + energy for cell

In cellular respiration glucose is broken down to produce carbon dioxide and water. This process releases energy. Oxygen breathed in from the air must be present.

Each anabolic or catabolic process usually involves a series of reactions. Each of these series is called a pathway. The combination of all the catabolic and anabolic reactions within a cell or an organism is called its metabolism.

DNA AND RNA

Nucleic acids are complex molecules that store genetic (inherited) information within cells. This information controls the growth, function, and reproduction

BIOLOGICAL DETERGENTS

Biological detergents contain enzymes that break down dirt and stains containing fats and proteins. These stains include food and sweat. The enzymes that are used include lipases to break down lipids (fats and oils) and proteases to break down proteins.

A granule of biological laundry powder magnified many times. Enzymes help digest fat and protein stains present in clothing.

INSECT SKELETONS

The hard external skeleton of insects such as this hissing cockroach, as well as crustaceans such as crabs and shrimps, contains a polymer (long chained molecule) called chitin. Chitin also occurs in the cell walls of fungi and is one of the most abundant substances on Earth.

? The molecules of life include lipids, carbohydrates, and proteins. Can you figure out where you would find these molecules in your own body?

of the cells and of the whole organism. There are two types of nucleic acid, deoxyribonucleic acid (DNA) and ribonucleic acid (RNA).

THE STRUCTURE OF DNA AND RNA

Scientists discovered the structure of DNA in the 1950s after x-ray diffraction was first used to look at the atomic structure of crystals and led to the science of molecular biology.

The pattern produced by x-rays passing through crystals revealed the

CYSTIC FIBROSIS

Cystic fibrosis is a disorder that people inherit from their parents. Its effects include making the mucous linings of their lungs thick and sticky, so they have trouble breathing. Its cause is thought to be a fault in a gene (segment of DNA).

The affected gene controls the production of a protein called CFTR (cystic fibrosis transmembrane conductance regulator). If someone has cystic fibrosis, this protein lacks the amino acid phenylalanine. The faulty protein upsets the salt balance of the lung cells.

positions of the atoms inside the crystals. Both DNA and RNA are long chains of molecular units called nucleotides. Each nucleotide consists of a sugar; a ring of carbon, nitrogen, and hydrogen atoms called a base; and a phosphate. A phosphate is a combination of phosphorus and oxygen atoms.

In DNA the sugar in the nucleotides is called deoxyribose. The DNA molecule has two chains of nucleotides coiled around each other in a double helix. The bases of one chain are joined to the bases of the other.

Ribose is the sugar in RNA nucleotides, and a molecule of RNA forms a single long chain.

There are four types of bases in DNA, and each base contains a different combination of carbon, nitrogen, and hydrogen atoms. These bases are called adenine (A), guanine (G), cytosine (C), and thymine (T).

In RNA the bases are adenine (A), guanine (G), cytosine (C), and uracil (U). DNA and RNA bases function in groups of three, called triplets. A string of triplets (such as AAA GAG ACA CCT) is said to "code" for a particular protein. In this way the triplet code dictates which proteins are produced in cells.

BIOLOGICAL PLASTICS

Some bacteria living in soil produce grains of chemicals called PHAs (polyhydroxyalkanoates). The bacteria use these chemicals as an energy supply.

Scientists have discovered that PHAs can be turned into plastics and made into bottles and other products. These plastics are biodegradable (they will break down naturally). After use the plastics can be buried in the ground. Soil bacteria then break down the plastics into carbon dioxide and water in around five weeks.

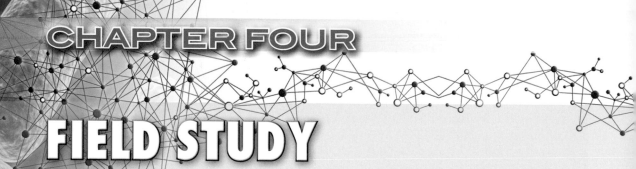

CHAPTER FOUR

FIELD STUDY

Studying organisms in the field is one of the most interesting and challenging areas of biology.

Millions of organisms belonging to thousands of species can make up a habitat such as a forest, and a variety of field methods are needed to study them and their environment. In order to study a science subject such as chemistry, the chemicals must be studied in the laboratory. In astronomy astronomers can only make observations from a distance. However, in biology it is often better to study interactions of organisms in their surroundings rather than removing

School children on a field trip collect biomass samples from the Rouge River in Michigan.

them to study in the laboratory.

The results of simple field studies, if they are properly done, can be important locally, nationally, or even globally. Local wildlife and conservation groups may be interested to know if there are individuals of rare species in your area. On a long-term project you could obtain information about changes in the numbers of certain types of organisms across the year or from year to year. These data may be used for national and global conservation plans.

USEFUL ITEMS FOR FIELD TRIPS

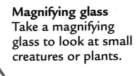
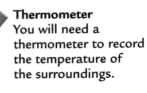

Magnifying glass
Take a magnifying glass to look at small creatures or plants.

Measuring tape
You will need to measure lengths of samples using a measuring tape.

Clipboard
Record all the information you collect on paper fixed to a clipboard.

Thermometer
You will need a thermometer to record the temperature of the surroundings.

Rain gauge
Find the amount of rainfall over a day or longer using a rain gauge.

Jar with lid
Put small creatures in a jar with air holes in the lid, then return them to their habitat.

TESTING HYPOTHESES

A biologist might observe that lizards seem to eat more prey on warmer days. Such a statement is called a hypothesis, and a biologist decides on a method to test it. In this case it could be counting the number of prey items eaten by lizards during warm and cool periods.

Sometimes studies are carried out in the laboratory, where conditions can be better controlled. A factor such as temperature is changed, and the effect on the organism is recorded. To see if the factor being changed is the cause of any change in the

? How would you carry out an experiment to test the hypothesis that lizards consume more food in warmer conditions? Think about what factors you would need to keep the same and about the kind of data that you would collect. How might you design the control experiment?

TEST YOUR HYPOTHESIS

Visit a local woodland, and construct a hypothesis relating the effect of the amount of light on the length of leaves of a species of plant. Test your hypothesis by measuring samples of leaves in shady and bright locations, and compare the lengths for the two places.

results, another experiment is carried out in which the factor is kept constant and the results are compared. That experiment is the control.

DO NO HARM

As a field biologist studying natural habitats, it is your duty to use responsible methods. When you visit a site and collect data, it is important to use nondestructive methods. Biologists sometimes collect animals or plants as part of their field studies, although they try to avoid doing so. If you do, it is best to put them back in their habitat as you originally found them. If you must set traps, ensure that you use ones that will not hurt or kill. You also might need to obtain permission to visit a site or carry out field research.

Sometimes biologists do need to use destructive methods for sampling populations. Pitfall traps are laid containing fluid that kills and preserves bugs that fall into them. This makes sure that carnivorous insects do not eat the rest of the sample.

Alfred Russel Wallace (1823–1913) was a prominent naturalist who traveled to the Malay Archipelago and the

Field biologists use square frames called quadrats to record the numbers and types of animals or plants found in a set area. Quadrats are made of wood or wire.

Amazon. Wallace collected specimens on a scale that would be thought irresponsible today. However, his collections are still of value to biologists.

FIELD SAMPLES

There are many different factors to consider in field studies, and it is not usually possible to control them as you would in a laboratory experiment. A field biologist uses natural variation in environmental factors as the basis for study. Instead of setting up an experiment in which the amount of light is changed to find out the effect on plant growth, a field biologist might choose two sites: one in bright sunlight and the other in the shade.

It is important to choose places that minimize differences in other factors, such as soil conditions, so you can be more certain the amount of light is the principal factor involved.

Some field studies look at single species. For example, how many individuals of a particular species are there in an area? Other studies are concerned with counting the number of species present in the area. It is not usually possible to count all the organisms since there are often just too many of them. Instead,

SAMPLING SMALL GROUND INVERTEBRATES

You can sample small ground invertebrates by setting pitfall traps. Dig small holes just big enough to hold polystyrene cups, ensuring that their rims are level with the soil surface. Leave them overnight, and see if you can identify the animals that you have caught the following morning. A small piece of stone or wood angled carefully over each trap will prevent flooding by rain.

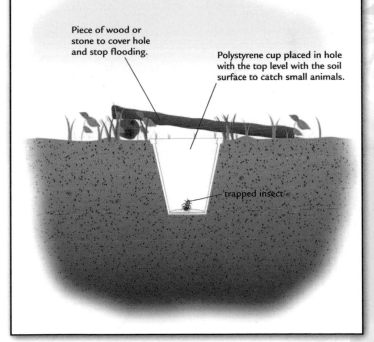

Piece of wood or stone to cover hole and stop flooding.

Polystyrene cup placed in hole with the top level with the soil surface to catch small animals.

trapped insect

biologists take samples from parts of the area to represent it.

SAMPLING STRATEGIES

A sample is a small, manageable part of the environment. If you wanted to know how many snails there are in a grassland valley, you could count the number in a much smaller area as your sample, such as a square yard. You can

AVERAGES

How reliable is a sampling technique? You can find out by testing the technique. Get 50 small swimming invertebrates, such as water fleas (Daphnia), from a pet shop that sells fish. Put them in a pint of water. Then take ten samples, each of 2 tablespoons (2 tablespoons equal 1 fl oz.) Count the number of water fleas in each sample (replacing the sample once it is counted), and figure out the average number per fluid ounce. Multiply that value by 16 to get the number per pint. How close is this calculated value to the real value of 50?

use a wooden or wire frame called a quadrat for this.

The more snails there are in the environment, the more snails you are likely to find in your sample. Take lots of samples to be sure that your results are likely to be typical of the whole area. The sample positions should be random, not in any particular order or pattern, so that your results represent the whole valley.

A simple sampling technique is a timed search. The number of observed organisms is recorded while conducting an active search for them over a fixed period of time in the chosen area.

Sampling animals that move around is often difficult and may require some sort of trapping technique. One of the simplest methods for catching ground

FEED THE BIRDS

Set up a bird feeder in your garden. Find out which species of birds visit your garden, and learn how to identify them. You might need to get hold of a simple field guide to do this. On different days spend half an hour observing your feeder and recording the number of species and individuals that visit. Do different species visit at different times of the year? Does the type of food provided matter?

SURVEYS

Schools, clubs, or individuals can participate in surveys of animals and plants. Researchers at the University of Minnesota developed The Monarch Larva Monitoring Project. Volunteers conduct weekly monarch and milkweed surveys, measuring per plant densities of monarch eggs and larvae and milkweed quality. They complete forms on paper or over the Internet. Their findings are entered into a database, analyzed, and presented as tables or charts.

Some web sites have guides, pictures, and audio samples to help identification for surveys. Projects like this give people experience in research.

invertebrates like beetles involves digging pitfall traps. Burrowing invertebrates can be caught by laying planks of wood on the ground and looking under them at regular intervals. Larger animals, such as rodents, are trapped with devices with snap-doors and trip mechanisms.

Sometimes it is appropriate to find out how samples vary in different places. This is done with a transect, which is a

HOW TO PLAN A PROJECT

Field biology does not usually demand special equipment, so anyone can plan and carry out a simple field study, whether it is on a single species or a whole ecological community. When you plan a study, you should check any safety considerations. Then try to be clear about your aims.

• Visit the field site, which can be a garden or a forest, to become familiar with it.

• Ask some very simple questions about what you observe. For example, does the bracken fern grow most abundantly in forest clearings? Are there more species of birds in a seasonal forest than in an evergreen one?

• Choose an appropriate method for collecting samples. Are you sampling an area or a volume? Would it be easier to record a timed search or to set traps?

• Record your results clearly in a field notebook. Remember to note down the size of your sample unit, or your results will be meaningless. This means the time of your search, the area of your quadrat, or the volume of your container.

• To obtain results that are truly representative of the environment, you must take more than one random sample. You therefore need to repeat the activity. Biologists have ways of ensuring they have collected enough data to produce meaningful results. It is a good idea to take about twenty samples. This means doing twenty timed searches (on different occasions) or laying twenty quadrats.

LOOKING AT NIGHTTIME INSECTS

Set up a light trap in your backyard to check out nighttime insects. Make a frame with wood, and attach a white sheet to it. Put a flashlight behind the frame on a warm summer night. Nighttime insects will be attracted to the light and will land on the sheet.

Identifying insect species is often very difficult, but you can use a field guide to identify moths, beetles, lacewings, and other large groups. Record the number of moths attracted over an hour, and repeat on different nights. Do weather conditions or the cycle of the moon affect the numbers of moths you catch?

straight line marked along a habitat using string or tape. Organisms are recorded at intervals along the line to find out how changes in conditions affect the species found at each interval. Transects produce interesting results when used for a gradual change in habitat such as from forest to forest clearing or down a seashore.

Many plants grow in a branching fashion, so it is better to determine the amount of area that they cover in the sample. Instead of recording the number of individual plants in an area, you can calculate the percentage cover.

SPECIES COUNTS

In a field study you could either be counting the number of individuals of one species or the number of different species present. For species counts you do not always have to put a name to each species, as long as you can tell that one organism belongs to a different species compared to another. Identification of species can be done using a field key. It is a series of statements or questions that leads you to the name of a species based on features of its appearance that can be easily observed. Keys are important for field work, and many have been published that cover a range of different groups.

STUDYING SNAIL POPULATIONS

Investigate a population of snails with a snail trap. Cut an orange in half, scoop out the fruit, and place the peel upside down on the ground. Look under the peel in the morning for snails. Mark each snail with a dot of correction fluid, then replace them under the peel. Use another trap a week later, and see how many marked snails return. This is called a mark–recapture experiment. It gives an idea of how large the population is.

TRACKING ANIMALS

Modern biologists are more concerned with the behavior of living organisms in

COVERINGS

Look at algae, mosses, and lichens on walls or gravestones. Design a project that investigates patterns in how they are distributed. You can sample these organisms by determining percentage cover. Finding the date on a gravestone can give you the maximum amount of time it has taken for the plants to have reached their current extent of cover.

the natural environment and use tracking techniques to study them. Radio and satellite tracking methods allow the investigation of moving animals from a distance. These methods are used to study patterns of movement and activity. They can be applied to discover other details of the animal's biology, such as

COUNTING PLANTS

Mark out a 10 ft x 10 ft (3m x 3m) grid on an area of grassland. Make a count of the number of species of plants growing in this area. You don't need to put names to the species to do this, but a simple plant guidebook will help you if you want to take this further. Figure out how many of each species there are (their abundance) by either counts of individuals or percentage cover. How do different species vary in their abundance?

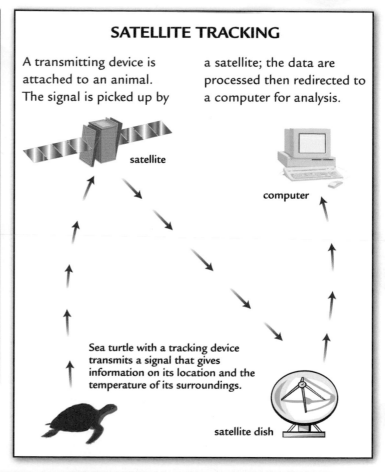

SATELLITE TRACKING

A transmitting device is attached to an animal. The signal is picked up by a satellite; the data are processed then redirected to a computer for analysis.

satellite

computer

Sea turtle with a tracking device transmits a signal that gives information on its location and the temperature of its surroundings.

satellite dish

HOW MANY SPECIES?

How many species of insects are there in an area of rainforest? In the 1970s Terry Erwin (born 1940) sampled the beetles from 19 trees of one species in a locality in Panama. He found 1,200 species of beetles! Some of these kinds of beetles are probably only found on this one kind of tree. On that basis Erwin estimated that there are around 12,500 beetle species and possibly more than 41,000 arthropod species (insects, spiders, and their relatives) in two and a half acres of Panamanian forest. If you extend this to the world's rainforests, they could be home to as many as 30 million species of forest arthropods. Of course, these estimates are only based on the rainforests of Panama. Some biologists think that 30 million species is an overestimate; others think there might be more. Further field studies need to be carried out in rainforests to get more accurate estimates of numbers of species living there.

DAMAGE

Biologists use field methods to find out about damage caused by some pest organisms. Rabbits are very destructive to crops and natural habitats. Enclosures are set up top exclude foraging rabbits. By looking for grazed plants, sampling methods are used to see if excluding rabbits reduces damage compared to a control site that rabbits can enter.

the size of its home range or its choice of habitat. In radio tracking the animal is tagged with a device that transmits a signal that is picked up by the antenna of a receiver and heard through headphones. It is important to know the geographical position of the receiver to fix the relative position of the tagged animal. This can be determined using signal strength and direction.

In satellite tracking the signal from the animal goes through to a satellite.

MAKING TRACKS

Sometimes novel field methods are called for when studying animals. There are only around 50 Javan rhinoceros in a reserve in western Java. They are very secretive animals and are rarely seen in the thick forest. Estimates of numbers of rhinos have been based on tracks left by the animals. From the sizes of footprints biologists have determined the presence of a nursing mother and calf. This is evidence that a breeding population exists in this reserve. Other evidence biologists might look for includes nests, dung, and remains of food.

EVIDENCE

You can get evidence of rarely seen animals passing through an area by finding their tracks or dung.

	Fox	Rabbit	Deer
Tracks			
Dung			

CHAPTER FIVE

LABORATORY WORK

Field methods are very important, but biologists also study living organisms closely in laboratories.

Most biologists use a "toolkit" of methods in the laboratory, from simple chemical tests to complex forms of modern microscopy. Laboratory work is vital in many real-life situations. For example, physicians examine samples from their patients to help diagnose illnesses, while

> Always do laboratory experiments with a qualified adult, such as your science teacher.

A teacher carries out a science experiment with his students. They are all wearing protective eyeglasses.

forensic scientists in police laboratories use many different tests to link suspects with a crime scene.

LAB SAFETY

Laboratories can be very dangerous places because most contain harmful chemicals and scientific apparatus that can cause injury or even death. Health and safety are always the first things to think about before carrying out any laboratory experiment. The basic rules are to act sensibly at all times (never play or run around in a laboratory), wear protective clothing (including eyeglasses), and follow all instructions very carefully. Never

perform experiments without the supervision of your biology teacher.

LAB EQUIPMENT

Equipment in the laboratory includes microscopes, scales for weighing, and centrifuges.

KEEPING THINGS CLEAN

It is important to always wash out the glassware you use in a laboratory. One reason is simply to keep things clean and tidy. Can you think of other reasons why it is important to wash things out before you do experiments?

Students use microscopes in a laboratory to examine objects that are too small to be seen with the naked eye.

THE FIRST MICROSCOPES

Microscopes were invented toward the end of the 16th century by the Danes Hans Jansen (1580–1638) and Hans Lippershey (1570–1619). It was a Dutchman, Anton van Leeuwenhoek (1632–1723), who pioneered the idea of using them to study life. Leeuwenhoek stumbled on microscopy while developing glass lenses as a hobby and later used the lenses to observe many living processes. One of his studies involved the way in which red blood cells move through the tiny blood vessels in a rabbit's ear.

OPTICAL MICROSCOPES

Most laboratory microscopes enlarge things from about 10 times to 1,500 times normal size. Optical microscopes use light, and they make a magnified image of the light rays reflected off, or transmitted through, the sample being studied. A slice of the sample is put on a glass slide underneath the lens.

SEEING IN GREATER DETAIL

The optical microscope helps scientists study tiny structures such as cells. The

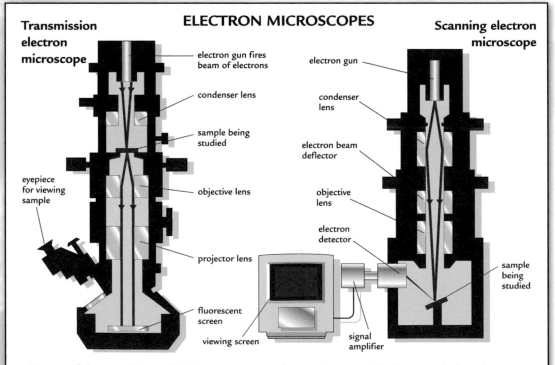

ELECTRON MICROSCOPES

Beams of tiny particles called electrons are used to study materials. A transmission electron microscope fires an electron beam through a thin slice of a sample. Lenses focus and magnify the image. A picture results on a fluorescent screen. A scanning electron microscope looks at solid objects rather than thin slices. A beam of electrons scans the sample's surface. Electrons scattered by the object are detected to build up an image of the sample on a viewing screen.

electron microscope shows smaller details, such as individual parts of cells. It uses an electron beam to view the samples and can magnify a million times.

HIGH SPEED MIXING

A centrifuge separates a mixture of substances by spinning them at very high speeds, much as a washing machine spins wet clothes. Some of these substances are heavier than others. Centrifugal forces pull these heavy substances to the bottom of the centrifuge tube, so the lighter substances stay close to the top.

The most powerful centrifuges, called ultracentrifuges, separate substances using forces up to half a million times greater than the pull of gravity. They were developed around 1920 by the Swedish chemist Theodor Svedberg (1884–1971). He used them to figure out the weights of protein molecules.

SEPARATING BLOOD

Blood consists of millions of tiny blood cells and fragments of blood cells (platelets) suspended in a yellow-colored fluid called plasma. Physicians often need to separate blood into its components either to diagnose illnesses or to give transfusions (replacements) of individual blood products to patients. A centrifuge is often used to process blood in this way.

Blood samples donated at a blood bank are refrigerated and stored until needed. Doctors use such samples for blood tranfusions.

CANCER SCREENING

Laboratory technicians use microscopes to examine samples from patients to find out if they have illnesses, such as cancer. This is a very skilled job, and it can be difficult to spot the abnormal cells that indicate cancer is present. Computerized "expert systems" are now being developed to detect cancer cells automatically. These systems should make diagnosis, quicker, cheaper, and more reliable.

ACCURATE WEIGHING

You can make more accurate measurements by weighing things a number of times and taking an average. Using any weighing device, try weighing an object, such as a single apple, 10 different times. Write down your measurement each time. Then add up the measurements, and divide by 10 to find a much more accurate weight.

STEELYARDS

Nurses weigh babies using steelyards. These scales have one pan suspended from a short arm and a much longer arm on the other side on which a weight slides along a measuring scale. Steelyards have changed very little since they were invented by the Romans around 2,000 years ago.

WEIGHING SAMPLES

Most laboratories have scales or balances. The simplest weighing machine has two pans—the object to be weighed is put in one pan, and weights are put in the other until the pans come to rest at the same level. Pan balances can be very accurate, but it is usually quicker and easier to use a balance that gives instant measurements on a digital readout.

Each paper circle, called a chromatogram, shows the different colors that make up some industrial dyes used for cloth. Scientists can tell what chemicals are in each color by the positions of the lines on the paper circles.

PAPER CHROMATOGRAPHY

1. Take a strip of blotting paper (a piece of coffee pot filter paper will do).

2. Using water-soluble marker pens, make two colored dots about 1/2 inch (1.25cm) from the bottom of the paper.

3. Hang the paper so the bottom just dips into a jug or beaker of water.

4. The ink in the marker is made from a number of different dyes. Each dye is attracted to water by a different amount and carried up the paper at a different rate. That is why the ink colors separate.

LAB METHODS

Different methods of analysis of substances and dissection of samples are some of the processes used in laboratories.

SEPARATING CHEMICALS FOR ANALYSIS

Chromatography is a way of separating different chemicals in a substance so that they can be analyzed. A sample is turned into a liquid or gas and allowed to move over a solid. The chemicals separate from one another as they travel at different speeds. Paper chromatography uses absorbent paper to separate the chemicals. Thin-layer chromatography uses a special type of glass. Uses of chromatography include analysis of chemicals in pollution and studying amino acids.

SEPARATING WITH ELECTRICITY

Electrophoresis is another way to separate parts of a substance. It uses electricity to make the different parts in the substance travel by different amounts. In one type of electrophoresis a sample, such as DNA, is placed at one end of a tray containing a chemically unreactive gel. Oppositely charged electrodes (electrical contacts) are then attached to either end of the tray. Different-sized pieces of DNA travel at different speeds and separate in the tray. The gel is treated so that the DNA fragments can be seen as a characteristic "ladder" pattern of bands.

DISCOVERING CHROMATOGRAPHY

Chromatography was first used by the Russian chemist Mikhail Tsvet (1872–1919) in 1906 to separate colors. He was trying to find out how chlorophyll in plants gives them their color. He dissolved green leaves in a solvent, poured the solution over a column of powdered chalk, and watched as colored bands started to form.

CRIME-SCENE INVESTIGATION

In a police laboratory scientists use gas chromatography to identify samples taken from a crime scene. A complex machine heats each sample so that it becomes a gas. The gas then flows past a specially absorbent solid packed into a coiled tube. The different chemicals in the gas travel at different speeds. The machine measures these speeds and draws a graph of them. The graph can be used to figure out what chemicals were originally in the sample. From these results the scientists can figure out what the sample might have been.

ROBERT KOCH

The technique of studying bacteria using nutrient media was perfected by the German physician Robert Koch (1843–1910). He studied microorganisms that cause diseases, including cholera, tuberculosis, typhoid, and anthrax. He won the Nobel Prize in 1905 and began the modern study of how bacteria cause disease.

PETRI DISHES AND NUTRIENT GELS

Bacteria are often specially grown in closed containers to be studied in a laboratory. The containers, such as petri dishes, are lined with a nutrient gel for the bacteria to feed on. With the lid removed from the dish, a small sample of bacteria is put on the gel. The lid is then replaced, and over a period of days or weeks the bacteria grow on the gel.

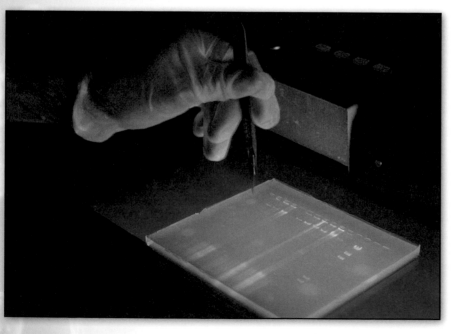

A scientist separates a sample of DNA using the process of gel electrophoresis.

DNA DATABASES

Many law enforcement agencies are now building up computer databases of the DNA fingerprints taken from suspects. Some people believe a great deal of crime could be stopped if the police stored a DNA fingerprint for everyone, not just criminals. Other people think that would be a violation of privacy and human rights.

BREAKING INTO PIECES

To understand how a living thing works, we often need to break it into pieces, much as a mechanic might dismantle an automobile. In biology the process of cutting apart a plant or animal to look at its structure is called dissection. It must be done with great care and with correct safety precautions so the parts inside the item being dissected are not damaged and can be studied.

DNA FINGERPRINTS

A DNA sample from a crime scene can be matched to a sample taken from a suspect using a technique called DNA fingerprinting since each person's DNA is unique. A sample is used to produce a DNA fingerprint using gel electrophoresis. If the two samples match, the suspect must have been at the crime scene.

In gel electrophoresis of DNA samples different-sized pieces of DNA travel at different speeds. The fragments are depicted as colored patterns of bands as seen on the transparencies held by this researcher.

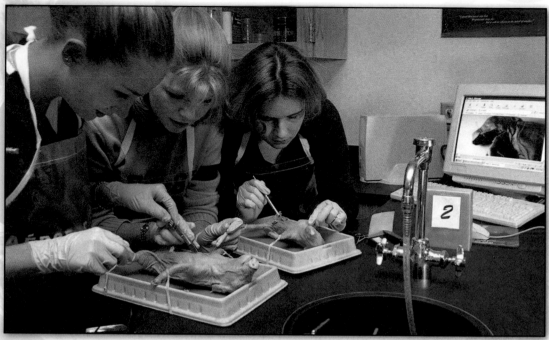

Students dissect pigs to examine their internal structure.

DISSECT A FLOWER

Try taking apart a flower very carefully. Either remove the petals with your hands, or ask an adult to help you use a sharp knife, or scalpel, to cut up (dissect) the parts inside. Be very careful with sharp tools. How many different parts of the flower can you identify? How many of each part does the flower contain? Why do you think there are so many parts?

ANIMAL TESTING

Scientists often perform experiments on animals that they cannot perform on people. Sometimes new drugs or medical procedures are tested on animals to make sure they are safe to use on humans. Scientists can find out more about the way human brains and visual systems work by studying those of animals, such as cats and monkeys.

AUTOPSIES

When people die unexpectedly, their bodies are sometimes dissected to find out what caused their death in a process called autopsy. During an autopsy a physician cuts apart the dead body and removes the main organs, which are weighed, examined carefully, and perhaps tested with other laboratory methods, such as microscopy or chromatography.

IS IT RIGHT TO USE ANIMALS?

Many scientists believe that it is essential to use animals in medical research. Without animal experiments, they believe, it would be harder to treat human illnesses, and many more people would suffer. Other scientists believe that it is cruel and wrong to use animals, especially for testing nonmedical products, such as cosmetics. They argue that animals have rights as well as people and should be treated with as much respect.

Another issue in the debate is that the results of an experiment on an animal may not be the same if it was carried out on a human. Perhaps, they argue, animals could be used only as a last resort, and other methods, such as testing using computer models, could be used instead wherever possible.

A costumed protester urges an end to animal testing.

NOTING RESULTS

Laboratory experiments are useful only if the results are recorded carefully because another scientist must be able to repeat your experiment to confirm the findings and add to what you have found. It is important always to make notes as you go along. Write down what you observe and any measurements you make. After the experiment write it all up fully. Include the method you used: the things you did and the exact order in which you did them. Next, write down the results of the experiment. Finally, write down what your conclusions are—the things you figured out from doing the experiment.

SETTING CONTROLS

All experiments need a control. A control proves that something happens for the reason you think it does and not for another reason. Suppose you have an idea that light helps plants grow. You could test this by placing one plant under a lamp and putting another in a dark cupboard. In this experiment, the plant in the cupboard acts as the control.

Water and feed both plants, and treat them in exactly the same way. After a few days, if the plant in the light grew more than the "dark plant," you would know it was the light that had made the plant grow because the plants were treated the same in every other way.

CHAPTER SIX

INTERPRETING THE DATA

These students use binoculars to identify and count the different birds that live in Glacier National Park, in Montana. Field data like these can be used to figure out the populations of different species in the area.

The process of studying the results of field and laboratory experiments is called data analysis. Data analysis involves drawing charts and producing statistics to help understand what the data mean.

When faced with a problem to solve, biologists develop a hypothesis, or untested idea. For example, a biologist might hypothesize that a large forest contains more types of beetles than a small patch of woodland. The biologist

INTERPRETING CHARTS

See if you can find a few examples of charts in newspapers, books, magazines, or on the Internet. What do the charts show? Are they just a simple count of something? Do they divide up something into different types? Can you figure out a hypothesis that explains why a chart appears the way it does? How would you test this?

BAR CHARTS

Suppose you wanted to show how deep different types of whales dive. You could draw a bar chart showing the depth each type of whale dives. The tallest bar would show the deepest dive. This bar chart shows that pilot whales dive the deepest.

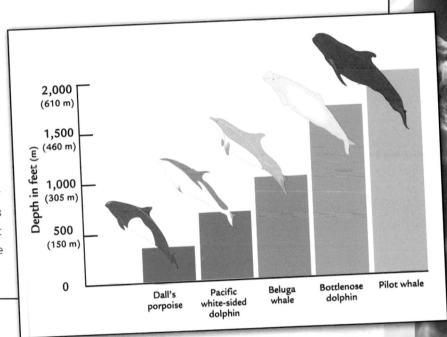

will carry out experiments. The measurements, or data, allow the biologist to test whether the hypothesis is true or false. This is called the scientific method.

Experiments are only ever as good as the quality of data that are collected. Even if several different things are compared, they must be measured in the same way. Suppose you are comparing the number of birds you see on different days of the week. You would need to spend the same amount of time watching for birds each day for the comparison to be fair. You would also need to make sure you did the experiment in the same place and at the same time each day. It would also be a good idea if the weather conditions were the same.

LINE CHARTS

You might be studying how Earth's temperature has changed over the last hundred years. You could draw a line graph with the year as the horizontal (x) axis and the difference between the global temperature and a long-term average as the vertical (y) axis. This graph slopes upward from left to right, suggesting that Earth's temperature has increased.

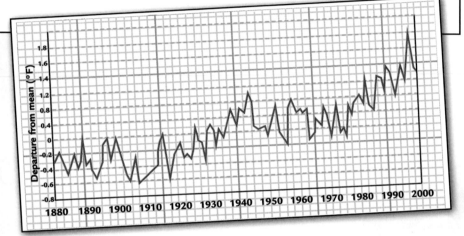

GRAPHIC ORGANIZERS

The data scientists collect in experiments can be presented in a range of ways. They could simply be written down in a table, perhaps, but that is not practical if a large number of meaurements have been made. Sometimes it helps to process the data after writing them down. For example, if you were counting birds each day, you could get three different people to write down separate counts of the birds and then take an average of those counts to produce a single, more accurate count for each day's bird-watching. Repeats of an experiment are called trials. In general, a higher number of trials leads to more accurate results.

The best way to show the results of an experiment is to draw a chart. There are many different types of charts, but the three most common are: bar charts,

PLOTTING CHARTS

You are a zookeeper, and you have 40 animals from North America, 20 from South America, 20 from Europe, 15 from Asia, and 5 from Antarctica. Draw a bar chart and a pie chart to show where the different animals come from. Which chart do you think is clearest?

PIE CHARTS

Suppose you want to know whether factories produce more polluting gases than, say, farms or businesses. You have data showing the volumes of gases given out by each source. You could add them up to figure out the total amount of gases produced. Dividing each source's volume by the total and multiplying by 100 gives the percentage each produces. You could then draw a pie chart, showing each source's figure as a slice.

Percentage of polluting gases produced from different sources

- Factories
- Automobiles/buses
- Homes
- Businesses
- Farms

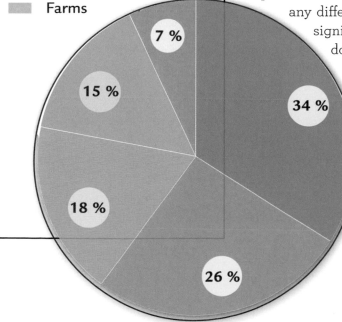

which show simple counts of things; pie charts, which show how one thing divides up into different types; and line charts, which show how one thing (called a variable) changes when something else also changes. All three types of charts are shown on these pages.

STATISTICS

Charts and graphs are important for presenting data and helping people understand their results. But to prove whether or not a hypothesis is true, biologists must use statistics. These mathematical procedures aim to show that the results are significant. This means that the data collected could not be a result of random chance. For example, suppose you wanted to know whether there were more birds around your neighborhood in spring than in summer. After collecting your data, you would need to produce some statistics to prove that any differences you had found were significant and not due to random chance. These statistics would allow you to prove your hypothesis.

There are many different statistical techniques. Some are simple and can be done with a calculator, but others are complex and need computer programs.

CHAPTER SEVEN

PUTTING DISCOVERIES TO WORK

GREEN REVOLUTION

In the 1960s some biologists began to try to solve the world's food shortages. Through selective breeding, scientists developed new varieties of crops like rice and corn that grew much faster and bigger than existing forms. These crops provided farmers with bumper harvests. There was such a dramatic rise in yields that people called it the Green Revolution.

Despite the introduction of these new types of crops to many parts of the developing world, the Green Revolution had little effect on world poverty. It was not applied in tandem with a political will to redistribute wealth. The crops were expensive to buy and maintain, and the poor remained unable to afford the food they were producing.

Discoveries made by biologists have had a profound effect on the way people live their lives.

Biological knowledge is essential in a range of fields, from medicine and agriculture to food preservation and conservation of fish stocks, from taking care of natural habitats and endangered species to making alcoholic drinks. Biology is also important in unexpected areas such as engineering, computing, and politics.

Rice strains developed during the Green Revolution produced much higher yields.

The earliest biological applications led to the development of agriculture, an advance that completely changed the way ancient peoples lived. Realizing that some plants grow from seeds, people sowed the first crops some time around 10,000 years ago. Animals such as cattle and sheep began to be domesticated—kept for their meat, hides, or milk—a few thousand years later. Ancient farmers soon discovered that features of their animals or crops were carried from one generation to the next. By sowing only the seeds of the best plants, farmers gradually changed the characters of their crops to suit their needs. This is called selective breeding. It led to the development of the many kinds of crops we see today.

Selective breeding also molded the characteristics of many domestic animals. Cattle, for example, were bred to produce more meat or milk. At the same time, tamer animals were chosen for breeding. This led to the gradual disappearance of the aggressiveness of the wild ancestors of these animals.

GENETIC MODIFICATION

Selective breeding can take a very long time, and there are no guarantees that desirable traits will pass from parent to young. With

FIGHTING PESTS

Biological research into the ways different organisms interact has inspired new ways of controlling pests in farming. Instead of fighting pests with toxic chemicals that can harm the environment, many farmers now enlist natural enemies to control pest numbers. This is called biological control.

Parasitic wasps are often used as biological control agents, targeting caterpillars, aphids, and other pest insects. A wasp lays an egg inside the pest. The egg hatches, and the young wasp eats the pest from the inside, killing it.

A detailed understanding of the biology of both pest and control agent is essential for a control program to be successful. Wasps are usually good biological control agents, since they tend to attack just one or a few closely related species. In the past, however, biological control programs were sometimes carried out without enough biological research beforehand. The introduction of predatory rosy wolf snails to control giant African land snails on several Pacific islands, for example, let to the extinction of dozens of native species of snails.

Parasitic wasp eggs have been laid in this caterpillar larva's body. The eggs will hatch and eat the larva. The wasp is a biological control agent, limiting the populations of damaging pest species.

These tomato plants have been genetically modified so their fruits last longer and contain more goodness than traditional varieties.

advances in biological understanding of genetics scientists realized that the genes of domestic organisms could be altered directly to improve yields or increase pest resistance. Scientists call this gene alteration genetic modification.

Another advance that may have dramatic consequences for agriculture is cloning. Scientists clone animals or plants by taking a cell from a parent and growing it into a new organism. A clone is genetically identical to its parent and should carry all of its desirable features. However, research suggests that cloned animals are susceptible to diseases such as arthritis. Cloning remains a highly controversial biological application.

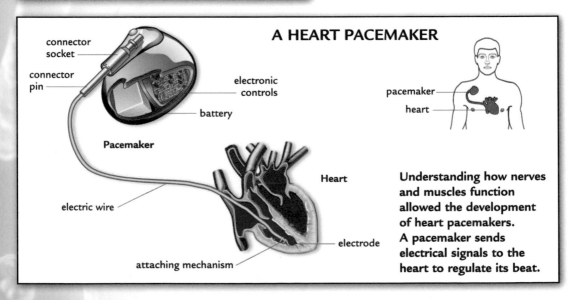

A HEART PACEMAKER

connector socket
connector pin
electronic controls
battery
Pacemaker
electric wire
attaching mechanism
Heart
electrode
pacemaker
heart

Understanding how nerves and muscles function allowed the development of heart pacemakers. A pacemaker sends electrical signals to the heart to regulate its beat.

INCREASING MEDICAL KNOWLEDGE

Advances in genetics have also revolutionized many medical fields, such as the treatment of genetic disorders like sickle-cell anemia. Medicine is rich in other biological applications. For many thousands of years medicine relied mainly on observation. People noticed that chewing bark from the cinchona tree fought malaria, for instance, but no one knew why. Healers were often regarded as workers of magic.

Today, medicine relies on a comprehensive understanding of the human body, from systems such as the nerves and organs such as the brain, liver, and

THE FIRST VACCINE

Edward Jenner (1749–1823) was an English physician. Like many 18th-century doctors, Jenner spent much of his time treating people afflicted with smallpox, a deadly disease common at the time. Jenner noticed that dairy farmers and milk maids did not catch smallpox. They had usually suffered from cowpox, though. Cowpox is a similar but non-deadly disease caught from cattle.

In 1796 Jenner decided to try using pus from cowpox sores to protect against future smallpox infection. He injected the pus into several patients, and each developed cowpox. Six weeks later Jenner injected the same patients with pus from smallpox sores. None of them showed symptoms of the deadly disease. Jenner had administered the first vaccination program. Sicne Jenner's discovery nearly two hundred years ago biological researchers have figured out how to vaccinate against many other diseases, inlcuding polio and TB.

Edward Jenner injects cowpox pus into a patient.

The bark of the Pacific yew tree contains taxol, an anticancer drug. The trees are rare, and to date biochemists have been unable to synthesize taxol in large quantities.

keep the heart beating regularly. Understanding of the immune system—the internal defense system of the body—allows doctors to administer vaccines that boost people's resistance to viruses and bacteria.

Knowledge of anatomy (the structure of body parts) helps physicians diagnose disease and perform surgery.

DRUG RESEARCH AND DEVELOPMENT

Although even experts do not understand precisely how many drugs function, the development of modern drugs is guided by an understanding of how the body works at a molecular level. If medical scientists know how the body's cell messaging system works, for instance, they can design drugs based on hormones, the body's natural chemical messengers. Many drugs are developed from natural chemicals. Taxol, for example, is an effective anticancer drug that was discovered in the bark of Pacific yew trees. Chemicals called alkaloids extracted from the leaves of the Madagascar periwinkle plant are an effective anti-leukemia drug. Following the introduction of these plant extracts, the survival rate of children with leukemia rose from 20 to 80 percent. Cases like this are often cited as a good reason to preserve biodiversity; there might be many more important drugs in as yet undiscovered rainforest plants.

Producing large quantities of drugs by harvesting wild plants is usually

kidneys down to individual cells and molecules. Knowledge of the electrical messages passed between nerves and muscles allows medical researchers to design artificial devices such as heart pacemakers.

A heart pacemaker mimics the electrical activity of nerves and muscles. The device sends out electrical impulses that

LEARNING FROM WORMS

Sometimes, a biological discovery can lead to major advances in other fields. Recently, biologists looking closely at the spines of the sea mouse made a remarkable discovery. The sea mouse is a type of worm that lives on deep ocean floors, where there is little light. To advertise its presence to potential mates, the sea mouse must use every scrap of light available.

Within sea mouse spines is a hexagonal arrangement of crystals that reflects light with near 100 percent efficiency. Such efficiency dwarfs the abilities of synthetic structures that engineers have designed to carry light. Fiber-optic cables, for example, enable communication over long distances. Information travels along them as pulses of light, but the signal must be regularly boosted due to the inefficiency of the cables.

The discovery of the properties of sea mouse spines may soon lead to a revolution in fiber-optic technology. The crystalline structure of the spines might be copied in future cables.

impractical. Scientists instead use their knowledge of biochemistry to synthesize (artificially produce) promising new drugs in the laboratory.

BIOLOGICAL MODELS

Just as the fruits of biological research are finding more and more applications, so other sciences are turning to biology for inspiration. In computing, for instance, the term *virus* is used to describe a program that attacks other computers in the same way that biological viruses attack people's bodies. Computer viruses even produce copies of themselves to increase their numbers, as do biological viruses. Computer scientists look at biological models, too, in search of new ways to build computers. "Neural networks," for example, are groups of connections that mimic the way nerve cells link together

BIOMIMETICS

The term *biomimetics* (life-mimicking) was coined to describe design and engineering inspired by the natural world. Many natural structures and materials evolved to cope with challenges of size, shape, and force distribution similar to those that human engineers face.

A tree trunk must be flexible enough to bend in the wind without breaking, for instance, but it must also support a huge weight. Similar problems must be dealt with when designing a bridge, for example.

Biomimetics research assumes that millions of years of evolution have produced good solutions to engineering problems in living organisms and attempts to copy them. The designer of the Eiffel Tower, for instance, analyzed and copied the shape of lines of load-bearing forces in human leg bones. In 1948 the swiss engineer George de Mestral (1907–1990) took a look at the cocklebur seeds that stuck to his clothes after a walk in the woods. Copying their hooks, de Mestral went on to invent Velcro fastenings.

There are many current fields of biomimetic research. For example, sonar-guided robots that find their way in the dark using ultrasound are based on the sonar used by dolphins and bats. Much biomimetic research is focused on finding new materials for use in manufacture. For example, composites consist of several layers of materials, each with different properties, that provide strength and flexibility. Many natural materials, such as bone and the shells of mollusks, are composites, as are synthetic materials like fiberglass.

Engineers try to measure stress and strain in composite materials just as insects do. These animals use sense organs to detect strain in their hard outer casing, a composite material called the exoskeleton.

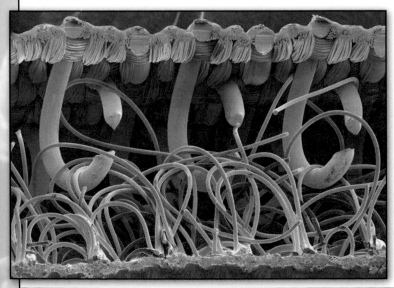

These are Velcro hooks. They are very similar to those found on the seeds of plants like cocklebur.

INSECT CRIME FIGHTERS

Biological knowledge can prove important in some surprising fields. Following a suspicious death, police investigators often require the help of forensic entomologists. These biologists specialize in identifying different types of insects on a corpse.

Insects such as flesh flies and carrion beetles lay their eggs on a corpse at specific times after death. The speed of the insects' development is regulated by temperature. So, by figuring out which insects are present and which stage of development they have reached, and by recording the temperature, forensic entomologists can make a good estimation of when a person died—a crucial detail in a murder investigation.

Adult carrion beetles on the dead body of a chipmunk. These beetles lay their eggs on corpses, including those of people, after they have begun to decompose (rot). The larvae (young) feed on the remains after they hatch.

in the human brain. By using neural networks, computers can learn from experience, just as we do, and build their own networks.

Scientists are researching the use of strands of DNA in computing. DNA is a molecule that acts as a code, driving the way a cell develops. DNA may soon be incorporated into "biochips" capable of storing billions of times more information than the silicon chips of today.

Biomechanics researchers study forces, movement, size, and shape. Biomechanical principles are important in a range of fields, including engineering and aviation. Biomechanicists also play an important role in accident investigation, helping determine the speed of a crashed automobile, for example.

One branch of biomechanics, called ergonomics, has revolutionized the design of many objects, from chairs and coffee pots to steering wheels and fishing rods. By looking at the movements, stresses, and strains of the human body, ergonomicists design objects to maximize comfort, efficiency, and ease of use.

CHAPTER EIGHT

BIOGRAPHY: ALEXANDER FLEMING

Alexander Fleming was a botanist, pharmacologist, and biologist best known for his discovery of the antibiotic penicillin.

A century ago, people stood at high risk of dying of an infectious disease or of infection after undergoing surgery. The accidental discovery of penicillin by Scottish bacteriologist Alexander Fleming led to the development of effective treatment of disease through bacteria-destroying chemicals called antibiotics.

Alexander Fleming was born on August 6, 1881, in the small village of Lochfield, Ayrshire, in southwestern Scotland, where his father owned a large farm. Alexander was the seventh of eight children. He went to school at nearby Kilmarnock Academy, but in 1894 his father died and Alexander's eldest brother inherited the farm. Another brother, Tom, had set up as a physician in London, and Alexander went to live with him, leaving school at age 16 to find work as a shipping clerk in a London office.

In 1902 each of the brothers and sisters inherited a small bequest of money from an uncle. Encouraged by Tom's

KEY DATES

1881	Born on August 6 in Lochfield, Ayrshire, Scotland
1894	Fleming's father dies; Alexander moves to London
1900	Enlists in the army
1902	Begins studies at St. Mary's Hospital Medical School, part of London University
1906	Graduates from medical school
1914–18	Serves in the Royal Army Medical Corps
1920	Appointed director of the Department of Systematic Bacteriology and assistant director of the Inoculation Department at St. Mary's
1922	Discovers lysozyme, a protein that kills bacteria
1928	Becomes professor of bacteriology at St. Mary's and lecturer at the Royal College of Surgeons; discovers penicillin
1929	Publishes results of work with *Penicillium* mold
1944	Is knighted to become Sir Alexander Fleming
1945	Shares the Nobel Prize for physiology or medicine with Ernst Chain (1906–1979) and Howard Florey (1898–1968)
1955	Dies on March 11

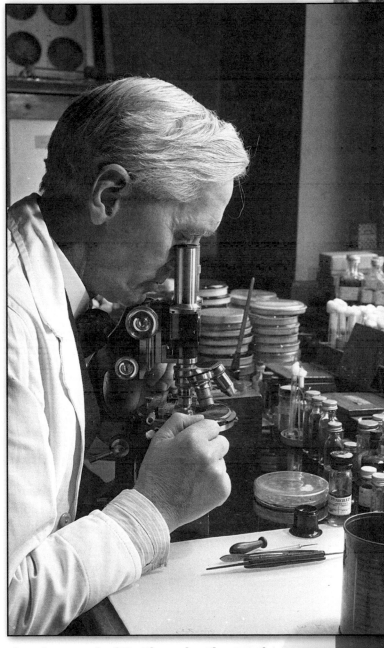

This photograph of Sir Alexander Fleming shows him in his laboratory studying bacteria cultures through a microscope. He spent his entire career at St. Mary's Hospital in London, and he was professor of bacteriology there for 20 years.

example, Alexander decided to invest his share in studying medicine. He performed outstandingly well in the qualifying examinations for medical school and chose to go to St. Mary's Hospital Medical School, part of London University. He graduated in 1906 and spent the rest of his career at St. Mary's Hospital.

THE EARLY YEARS OF BACTERIOLOGY

Fleming started to specialize as a surgeon, but he was soon persuaded to switch to bacteriology. This is the branch of science devoted to the study of the tiny organisms called bacteria that live in water, soil, or the bodies of plants and animals. Some are harmless, or even beneficial, to their hosts, but others produce toxins (poisons) that damage tissue, causing infection and disease. German physician Robert Koch (1843–1910) and French chemist Louis Pasteur (1822–1895) had led the way in isolating specific disease-causing bacteria—for example, those responsible for causing anthrax, tuberculosis, chicken cholera, and rabies—and in developing vaccines to provide immunization against them.

THE SEARCH FOR A "MAGIC BULLET"

German bacteriologist Paul Ehrlich (1854–1915) is considered to be the founder of chemotherapy, the use of toxic chemical agents to attack the causes of disease. Ehrlich studied medicine at the University of Leipzig in Germany. He also loved chemistry, which he had taught himself while a student. Scientists had recently learned how to make synthetic dyes using chemical reactions. It was found that such dyes could be used to stain bacteriological specimens so that they are visible under a microscope. This fascinated Ehrlich, giving him an area of research that combined his interests in biology and chemistry.

In 1884 Ehrlich became professor at the Charité Hospital in Berlin. While there he found a way to stain white blood cells. He also succeeded in staining the bacillus that causes tuberculosis, but as a result of his laboratory work, he developed tuberculosis himself. Once restored to health, he was invited by Robert Koch in 1890 to join his team at the Institute of Infectious Diseases at Berlin. Also working there were German bacteriologist Emil Adolf von Behring (1854–1917) and Japanese bacteriologist Shibasaburo Kitasato (1856–1931), who had developed a serum, or antitoxin, against diphtheria. Ehrlich worked with them on ways of making the serum more effective.

In 1896 an Institute for the Investigation and Control of Sera was established at Steglitzin, Germany. Ehrlich was appointed director. There he started to pursue a line of reasoning that arose out of his interest in stains. For a stain to attach itself to a cell, it must combine chemically with something in the cell. This usually resulted in the death of the cell. Erhlich therefore began the search for a dye that would look for, stain, and then kill harmful bacteria without affecting healthy cells. Such dyes would be what he called "magic bullets."

WHAT IS IMMUNIZATION?

Immunization is a way of producing increased resistance to infection. This is done by stimulating the production of antibodies, part of the body's defense mechanism against disease. Antibodies are protein molecules produced by white cells in the blood in response to the presence of foreign molecules (antigens) produced by invading disease-causing bacteria; they combine chemically with the antigens and make them harmless.

Somebody who has recovered from an infectious disease such as measles or chickenpox will have natural immunity against future attacks of that disease because the antibodies made during the first attack persist in the blood stream. A mother passes on the antibodies in her blood stream to her baby before it is born, and these will protect the infant during the first months of life.

Immunization against a specific disease can be artificially induced by introducing antibodies from an infected person or animal into the blood stream to stimulate the development of the antibodies

Robert Koch (seated center at the table) was a founding figure of bacteriology, who isolated the organisms responsible for anthrax, tuberculosis, and cholera. He is seen here on an expedition made to East Africa in the early 1900s to investigate sleeping sickness and other tropical infectious diseases.

to fight it. The recipient may develop the disease, but usually in a mild form. This is known as vaccination or inoculation, and was first used against smallpox in the 18th century. In 1891 the German government established the Institute of Infectious Diseases in Berlin with Robert Koch at its head, and it was there that German bacteriologist Emil von Behring (1854–1917) developed a form of immunization known as serum therapy. Serum is a clear, yellowish fluid that is part of the composition of the blood. Behring found that injections of blood serum containing antibodies from an animal suffering from tetanus will confer immunity to the disease in other animals. Further experiments showed that the same was true for diphtheria, an acute bacterial disease, much more common then than it is today, that leads to extreme difficulty in breathing. Behring was able to develop a serum vaccine to immunize humans against diphtheria.

First used in 1891, it brought about a dramatic fall in the death rate from the disease. Immunization was a powerful tool in preventing the spread of diseases. But bacteriologists had yet to find a way to destroy bacteria causing infection within the body and bring about the recovery of seriously ill patients. Although several antibacterial agents (chemicals that kill bacteria) had been found by the early 20th century, all were known to have harmful effects on human tissue.

WAR AND DISEASE

Fleming began working in the bacteriological laboratory at St. Mary's under Sir Almoth Wright (1861–1947), who had developed a vaccine against typhoid fever. He soon became interested in Ehrlich's development of chemotherapy and pioneered the use of salvarsan by intravenous injection (into a vein).

In 1914 the nations of Europe were plunged into four years of war. Fleming served in the army medical corps throughout World War I. Many soldiers died from simple flesh wounds because doctors were unable to prevent bacterial infection from spreading through the body and causing major infections such as septicemia (blood poisoning). Fleming became more determined than ever to find a substance that would destroy harmful bacteria.

After the war Fleming returned to St. Mary's Hospital. He started to investigate various secretions of the body for their effects, if any, on bacteria. In 1922 he discovered lysozyme, an enzyme (protein molecule) present in tears and saliva. Fleming was able to establish that lysozome has some bacteria-destroying power.

THE ANTIBACTERIAL MOLD

In 1928 Fleming, by now professor of bacteriology at St. Mary's, made his most famous discovery. He had made a culture of bacteria on some petri

A casualty receives first aid in the field in World War I. Weapons caused mutilation on an unimaginable scale, medical treatment was frequently carried out without painkillers, antiseptics proved ineffective, and simple infections often killed.

dishes, and when he had finished with some of the samples, he piled the dishes in the sink, where he left them uncovered. Several days passed before he got around to cleaning the dishes, and when he did he noticed specks of green mold on the agar gel. This was fairly common, but he also noticed that there was a bacteria-free circle around each speck of mold: the bacteria in the area around the mold had been killed. This was most unusual behavior and, try as he might, Fleming was never able to repeat the finding.

Eventually Fleming identified the mold as the fungus *Penicillium notatum*, a close relative of the mold that appears on stale bread. When he exposed a number of disease-causing bacteria to the mold he found that the mold killed some of them but left others unharmed. Fleming decided that the mold must be giving off a substance that was fatal to the bacteria, and he called this "penicillin." In fact, other scientists had also noticed this effect of *Penicillium notatum*, but Fleming was the one to realize its significance. "My only merit," he later said, "is that I did not neglect the observation and that I pursued the subject as a bacteriologist." However, he was not a skilled chemist, and he failed to isolate the penicillin from the mold. He reported his findings to the *British Journal of Experimental Pathology* (1929), but his paper aroused little interest and he abandoned his work on penicillin. Fortunately, he kept a sample of the unusual mold he had created.

HOWARD WALTER FLOREY 1898–1968

Howard Florey was born in Adelaide, Australia, where he qualified as a physician. In 1921 he won a scholarship to Oxford University in England; he became professor of pathology there from 1934 to 1962. Like Fleming, he investigated lysozyme, an antibacterial substance found in tears and saliva, and in 1939 joined German-born biochemist Ernst Chain (1906–1979) in investigating other antibacterial substances. One they chose was penicillin, which they were able to isolate and purify for clinical use. By May 1940 they were convinced of its effectiveness, andFlorey lobbied the American government and industries to ensure its mass production. Penicillin was used, with great effectiveness, in the treatment of casualties in World War II (1939–45).

In 1945 Florey shared the Nobel Prize for physiology or medicine with Chain and Fleming.

MEDICINE IN WAR

War, which had such devastating effects on military and civilian populations alike in the 20th century, nevertheless had an important impact on advances in medical science; it encouraged the introduction of new surgical techniques for treating wounds, and the development and testing of new drugs for controlling and treating disease.

TREATING THE WOUNDED

The conditions in which Fleming and other army surgeons worked at the front in World War I (1914–18) were appalling. French surgeon Alexis Carrel (1873–1944) developed, with English chemist Henry Dakin (1880–1952), a technique for continuously washing wounds with an antiseptic fluid, which helped control infection in field hospitals. X-rays proved important in locating bullets and shrapnel fragments in patients' bodies, and Marie Curie organized radiological services at the front.

Severe blood loss from wounds was common. In 1901 Austrian-born American pathologist Karl Landsteiner (1868–1943) had identified blood groups A, O, B, and AB, which improved the success of blood transfusions. Methods of keeping blood refrigerated led to the setting up of blood "banks," from which blood could be taken when needed.

Other developments addressed the longer-term damage suffered by service personnel. New Zealand-born plastic surgeon Harold Gillies (1882–1960) invented techniques to help victims of disfiguring wounds and burns. Specialties such as orthopedics (the study and repair of the spine and joints) and prosthesis (the fitting of artificial limbs) developed, while the new science of psychotherapy offered hope to those suffering the damaging psychological after-effects of war (often referred to as "shell-shock").

FIGHTING INFECTION

The spread of bacterial disease among fighting soldiers was a constant threat. The bacterium that causes tetanus is present in the soil; it usually infects victims through a wound and causes muscular spasms. After 1915 casualties were given the tetanus antitoxin as a matter of course. Among American troops the death rate dropped to 1 percent of what it had been in the American Civil War (1861–65). The United States also made vaccination against typhoid fever—caused by a bacterium carried in contaminated water—compulsory for its military personnel in 1911, bringing about a similar dramatic drop in death rates.

Armed services personnel were ideal subjects for large-scale clinical trials of new drugs. The introduction of penicillin early in World War II (1939–45) had a huge impact on the control of infection in casualties. Penicillin was not a cure-all, however; the antibiotic streptomycin, introduced in 1944, was the only treatment for tuberculosis.

Troops fighting in the tropics were at risk from another deadly disease: malaria. In 1939 the Swiss chemist Paul Müller (1899–1965) introduced a powerful insecticide, DDT, which kills the mosquitoes that carry it.

But although DDT was effective against several insect-borne tropical diseases, it was later banned because of its devastating effect on the environment.

The Northern Regional Research Laboratory of the U.S. Department of Agriculture was one of the organizations set up during World War II to research penicillin. Here researchers discuss their findings at a June 1944 conference.

THE ANTIBIOTICS REVOLUTION

Penicillin belongs to the group of chemical substances known as antibiotics. They are produced by living organisms, usually a microorganism, and have the ability to harm other microorganisms. Bacteria and fungi naturally release antibiotics into the environment. An antibiotic can kill bacteria or stop their growth, but it is only of medical value if it can do so without harming human cells. That was what alerted Chain and Florey to the possible beneficial effects of penicillin. Fleming had already carried out tests to see if penicillin was safe by exposing white blood cells to the mold. They were unharmed. One of Fleming's assistants grew a culture of *Penicillium notatum* in milk and was able to drink the moldy milk without any ill-effects. The discovery by Chain and Florey that penicillin could be isolated from the *Penicillium notatum* mold and used to destroy bacteria in the body without causing harm to human tissue heralded a revolution in the medical battle against disease.

ANTIBIOTICS GALORE

Penicillin was not, however, the first antibiotic to be commercially manufactured. Two years earlier, in 1939, René Jules Dubos (1901–1982) isolated a substance he called tyrothricin from a bacterium *Bacillus brevis* that lives in the soil. Dubos was a French-born microbiologist who became an American citizen in 1938. He had been investigating the antibacterial properties of soil microorganisms for some time. Tyrothricin proved to be effective against a number of bacteria, but unfortunately it also killed red blood cells, and proved too toxic for large-scale use.

Dubos's researches and techniques influenced the development of penicillin and aroused the interest of other scientists in soil bacteria. Tyrothricin was effective only against simple Gram-positive bacteria. Russian-born biologist Selman Waksman (1888–1973), professor of soil biology at Rutgers University in New Jersey, concentrated his search on substances that would attack the more harmful Gram-negative bacteria. He had discovered a soil mold called *Streptomyces griseus* as early as 1915, but did not finally succeed in isolating a substance from it, which he named streptomycin, until 1943. This was able to kill Gram-negative bacteria. It was a major medical breakthrough because it made it possible to manufacture an antibiotic specially targeted at tuberculosis bacteria, which are highly resistant.

Waksman was awarded the Nobel Prize for physiology or medicine for this work in 1952, and donated the prize money to a research foundation at Rutgers. With his research team he went on to discover several more antibiotics, including neomycin, which is used to prevent infection during intestinal surgery. Within a few years other researchers had isolated the "tetracyclines." These are six antibiotic compounds that were less toxic to the patient than streptomycin; they are used in the treatment of a variety of illnesses from eye infections to Rocky Mountain spotted fever.

RESISTANT STRAINS

Although antibiotics are used to treat bacterial and fungal infections, they are not effective against viruses, minute parasitic organisms that cause many diseases ranging from the common cold to viral meningitis. But a greater drawback to antibiotics is the resistance that bacteria may eventually develop to them. If an antibiotic does not kill all the bacteria causing disease in a patient, it is the more resistant bacteria that will survive and reproduce rapidly to pass their resistance on to others. Fleming noted this tendency as early as 1946 when he wrote "the administration of too-small doses [of penicillin] leads to the production of resistant strains of bacteria." Eventually bacterial infections may be resistant to one or even several antibiotics, making it necessary to discover new, stronger varieties.

NEW HOPE FOR CURING OLD DISEASES

Meanwhile, a further breakthrough in the war against infection was made by German biochemist Gerhard Domagk (1895–1964). Director of experimental pathology and bacteriology for the huge German chemicals company I. G. Farben, Domagk was interested in Erhlich's work on synthetic dyes and tested various dyes for their effectiveness against infections. In 1932 he found that a derivative of a dye used in the leather industry, Prontosil red, cured mice infected with streptococcal bacteria, responsible for a number of diseases including scarlet fever and other throat infections. It was soon realized that the active chemical ingredient of the drug was a compound called sulfanilamide. Two more related compounds, produced in 1938 and 1940, proved effective against pneumonia, and a third in 1941 was successful in treating an acute form of the brain infection meningitis. Known as sulfa drugs, they saved many lives in their early years of use.

THE EMERGENCE OF PENICILLIN

In 1935, two men, pathologist Howard Florey and biochemist Ernst Chain, who were working in the science laboratories of Oxford University, began researching antibacterial substances to control wound infection. Their work grew more urgent as the likelihood of another war in Europe drew closer. Both men were interested in investigating the antibacterial

ERNST BORIS CHAIN 1906–1979

British biochemist Ernst Chain was born in Berlin, Germany. He graduated in chemistry and physiology from the Friedrich Wilhelm Institute there, and then worked at the Institute of Pathology, Charité Hospital, Berlin from 1930 to 1933. In that year the anti-Jewish policies of Germany's new chancellor Adolf Hitler (1889–1945) forced him to flee to England. There he worked briefly at Cambridge University before moving to join Florey at Oxford University in 1935. Working together they were able to isolate penicillin and demonstrate its unique antibacterial properties.

After the war, having shared the 1945 Nobel Prize for physiology or medicine with Florey and Fleming, Chain became director of the International Research Center for Chemical Microbiology in Rome, where he stayed from 1948 to 1961. In 1954 he became involved with the pharmaceutical company the Beecham Group, and helped them develop a range of semi-synthetic penicillins.

In 1961 Chain returned to England, and was appointed professor of biochemistry at Imperial College, University of London. He held various senior posts there until 1979. He died in Ireland the same year.

properties of lysozyme, the enzyme Fleming had discovered 12 years earlier.

In 1938, after Chain came across Fleming's observations of the behavior of the *Penicillium notatum* mold, he and Florey decided to try to isolate the substance.This proved to be a long and difficult business, but eventually, after 18 months, Chain and Florey managed to extract 0.0035 ounce (100 mg) of penicillin in the form of a yellow powder. It was enough to conduct tests. They found that a solution of one part of the yellow powder in a million parts of a solvent prevented the growth of streptococci bacteria in mice. They went on to treat with pencillin more mice that had been given lethal doses of bacteria, and when these tests, too, proved successful, they published their results.

Now they decided to try the substance on a human subject. Their first patient was an Oxford police officer who was dangerously ill with septicemia. At first things went well, and the patient seemed to be recovering, but the researchers exhausted their supplies of penicillin before all the bacteria in his body had been destroyed. The infection took hold again and the patient died a month later.

Penicillin had, however, proved its effectiveness, and continued to do so in eight further successful tests on humans against a variety of infections. As always, the problem was maintaining a sufficient supply of penicillin, which Florey and Chain continued to make in their Oxford laboratory.

Production speeded up after the United States became involved in World War II in 1941, and arrangements were made for the American pharmaceutical industry to begin large-scale production of the drug.

By 1943 enough penicillin had been produced to allow it to be used for the first time to treat battlefield casualties in North Africa and Sicily.

Large quantities were ready in time to treat casualties in the D-Day battles in Normandy (June 1944). By this time penicillin had more than proved itself in combating bacterial infections, but it was not made available to civilians until World War II ended in May 1945.

SHARING THE NOBEL PRIZE

After his discovery of penicillin, Fleming had gone on to do other important work, identifying the organisms that infect wounds and developing new techniques for staining bacteria. He studied the effects of various disinfectants on different bacterial species and showed how streptococcal cross infections can occur in hospitals. In the 1960s Chain went on to discover penicillinase, an enzyme that some bacteria can learn to synthesize, which makes them resistant to penicillin.

Both Alexander Fleming and Howard Florey were knighted by King George VI (1895–1952) in 1944 for the part they had played in developing penicillin, and in 1945 Alexander Fleming, Howard Florey, and Ernst Chain shared the Nobel Prize for physiology or medicine.

Fleming retired in 1954. Although Florey and Chain had been responsible for penicillin's transformation into a usable drug, it was Fleming who had become identified in the public mind with its creation, resulting in the "Fleming myth," as he himself called it. After his death on March 11, 1955, he was buried in St. Paul's Cathedral, London.

SCIENTIFIC BACKGROUND

POLITICAL AND CULTURAL BACKGROUND

Before 1920

The German bacteriologist Robert Koch (1843–1910) isolates several bacteria, including those for the lung disease tuberculosis and the acute infection of the intestines, cholera

The German bacteriologists Paul Ehrlich (1854–1915) and Emil von Behring (1854–1917), and the

Japanese bacteriologist Shibasaburo Kitasato(1856–1931) develop an antitoxin against diphtheria, a disease that causes fever and breathing difficulties; Ehrlich later develops salvarsan (a compound of the poison arsenic) to treat syphilis

1920

1922 Fleming discovers that lyzosyme, a protein molecule in bodily fluids, helps the human body to limit bacterial infection

1922 The Ehrlich–Behring–Kitasato antitoxin has brought annual deaths from diphtheria down from 43.3 per 100,000 members of the population in 1900 to 14.6 per 100,000

1922 The 26 counties of southern Ireland sign a treaty with Britain to become the Irish Free State; the remaining six counties of Protestant Northern Ireland remain part of the United Kingdom

1925 The SS (*Schutzstaffel*) is founded as a personal bodyguard for German leader Adolf Hitler (1889–1945); its members will become ruthless enforcers of the Nazi regime

1925

1927 In the United States *The Jazz Singer*, starring Al Jolson (1886–1950), plays to amazed audiences; it is the first "talkie," featuring speech and music synchronized to the action

1928 Fleming observes mold of the fungus *Penicillium notatum* killing bacteria; he calls this antibacterial substance penicillin, but does not isolate it

1929 Fleming publishes his findings about *Penicillium* mold

1930 The first association football (soccer) World Cup is held in Uruguay; the final, between Uruguay and Argentina, is won 4–2 by the home team

1930

1932 The German biochemist Gerhard Domagk (1895–1964) finds the first "sulfa drug," a sulfonamide compound that can be used to treat bacterial infections

1932 Franklin Delano Roosevelt (1882–1945) is elected to the American presidency on his promise of a "New Deal" to bring the country out of economic recession

1933 In Germany the Nazis and their allies gain the power to rule without reference to the Reichstag (the Parliament); the Nazis go on to launch a campaign of persecution against German Jews

1935 In Oxford, England, Australian-born Howard Florey (1898–1968) and German-born Ernst Chain (1906–1979) begin work into antibacterial substances

1935

1935 At the Berlin Olympics in Germany, intended by Hitler to be a showcase of white Aryan supremacy, black American athlete Jesse Owens (1913–1980) wins four gold medals

1938 Domagk finds a sulfa drug that is effective against pneumonia

1937 The tragic last moments of the airship *Hindenburg*, which crashes in New Jersey killing 36 people, are dramatically conveyed to the public by a news reporter

1939 The French-born American bacteriologist René Jules Dubos (1901–1982) isolates the antibacterial substance tyrothricin from soil bacteria, but it is too toxic to be taken internally by humans

1939 Florey and Chain isolate and purify a small sample of penicillin

1939 World War II (1939–45) begins in Europe as German forces invade Poland on September 1; Britain and France declare war on Germany two days later

1940

1941 Domagk finds a sulfa drug that is effective in some cases of meningitis

1941 Pharmaceutical companies begin to produce penicillin for Allied troops

1943 In the United States the Russian-born biologist Selman Waksman (1888–1973), who has coined the term "antibiotic" for antibacterial substances such as penicillin, isolates streptomycin, the first antibiotic to be effective against tuberculosis

1943 The Clinton Engineer Works, later known as Oak Ridge, is built near Knoxville, Tennessee; it is the world's first operational nuclear reactor

1944 In the Soviet Union the siege of Leningrad by German troops finally ends in January; it has lasted 900 days and 900,000 of the city's 3 million inhabitants have died

1945 Fleming, Florey, and Chain share the Nobel Prize for physiology or medicine

1945

1946 Fleming reports that insufficient doses of penicillin lead to resistant strains of bacteria

1948 Researchers use penicillin to prevent bacterial contamination of experimental virus cultures

1949 Waksman isolates neomycin, which can be used to treat skin, eye, and bowel infections

1948 The Jewish state of Israel is proclaimed, with Chaim Weizmann (1874–1952) as president and David Ben-Gurion (1886–1973) as premier

1949 American boxer Joe Louis (1914–1981) retires undefeated after 12 years as world heavyweight boxing champion

1950

1952 Waksman wins the Nobel Prize for physiology or medicine for his discovery of streptomycin

1950 The Korean War begins as the Soviet-backed North Koreans launch an attack on the South. United Nations troops, dominated by American forces, try to repel the invasion; an armistice is eventually signed on July 27, 1953

1954 The U.S. Supreme Court rules that educating black and white people separately is unconstitutional; a growing civil rights movement is headed by Baptist minister Martin Luther King Jr. (1929–1968)

After 1955

1988 American chemists Gertrude Elion (1918–1999) and George Hitchings (1905–1998) and Scottish pharmacologist James Black (1924–) win the Nobel Prize for physiology or medicine for their work designing new drug treatments. Elion and Hitchings have developed

a range of "antimetabolites," including acyclovir, one of the first drugs to be used to treat a virus, herpes; while Black has produced "beta-blockers" for use in treating heart disease

amino acid Nitrogen-containing molecule that is a building block of proteins.

analogous When two structures on different organisms are similar but have evolved independently.

antibody Protein produced by white blood cells in response to an antigen; important in an immune response.

antigen Molecule on a foreign body that the immune system is able to recognize.

asexual reproduction Production of young without the need for mating or the fusion of sex cells.

atom The smallest particle of an element that can exist.

bacterium A single-celled organism that lacks a nucleus and organelles.

binary fission Type of asexual reproduction in organisms formed by single cells; one cell divides into two.

biodiversity The biological diversity in an area, as indicated by the number of different species of organisms.

biological control The use of predators and parasitoids (killer parasites) to control pest organisms.

biomechanics The study of biological forces.

biomimetics Branch of engineering that copies designs from the natural world.

cellulose Chemical that gives strength to plant cell walls.

centrifuge Machine that separates mixtures by spinning them at very high speeds.

chitin Substance that gives structural support to the exoskeleton of insects, as well as the walls of fungi.

cladistics Technique that compares large numbers of characteristics among species to build up a family tree.

classification The organization of different organisms into related groups by biologists.

clone Organism that is genetically identical to its parent and siblings.

coevolution Evolution involving changes in two species that depend on each other to survive.

community A group of different species that share a habitat.

control Part of an experimental technique. It proves the results are due to the feature under investigation.

convergent evolution When distantly related creatures evolve similar body plans in response to similar environments.

deoxyribonucleic acid (DNA) Molecule that contains the genetic code for all cellular (nonvirus) organisms.

dissection Cutting apart an animal or plant in order to study its structure.

ecosystem An ecological unit that comprises a community of organisms and its environment.

egg Female sex cell.

electrophoresis Technique for separating mixtures by passing an electric current through a sample.

enzyme Protein that speeds up chemical reactions inside an organism.

eukaryote cell Cell containing organelles; animals, plants, and fungi are eukaryotes.

evolution Process of change in groups of organisms over long periods of time.

exoskeleton Tough outer skin of animals such as insects, spiders, and crabs.

fertilization The fusion of a sperm with an egg.

forensic entomology The use of insects in police investigations.

gene Section of DNA that codes for the structure of a protein.

hemoglobin Pigment that occurs in red blood cells; binds to oxygen and carbon dioxide to carry these gases around the body.

homology The presence of shared characteristics in two organisms.

hormone Chemical messenger that regulates life processes inside an organism.

humor One of four liquids once thought to give organisms life.

hypothesis An idea that can be tested with an experiment.

lipid One of a group of molecules that form oils, fats, and waxes.

molecule Particle made of two or more atoms.

natural selection Theory that only the fittest organisms survive and reproduce. This is the driving force behind evolution.

nucleus Organelle that contains a eukaryote cell's DNA.

organelle Membrane-lined structures inside eukaryote cells, such as the nucleus.

polymer A long chain of molecules.

prokaryote cell Cell of a bacterium, which does not contain organelles.

protein Molecule formed by amino acids.

protist A single-celled eukaryote organism with a nucleus and organelles.

quadrat Square apparatus used for sampling.

ribonucleic acid (RNA) Chemical similar to DNA involved in protein production.

selective breeding The change of animals through the selection by people for desirable traits. It led to the development of the different breeds of domesticated and farmed plants and animals.

sexual reproduction Production of young through the fusion of sex cells, often after mating between a male and a female.

species A group of organisms that can potentially mate with each other to produce young that can also interbreed successfully.

sperm Male sex cell.

spontaneous generation Ancient belief that organisms could arise spontaneously from nonliving matter.

stromatolite Columnlike fossil formed by mats of bacteria in shallow ancient seas.

subspecies Subdivision of a species; a population that may have different colorings and a different range than other subspecies but can still interbreed with them.

vaccine Dead or harmless versions of a disease-causing organism that are injected into the body and allow the immune system to recognize the pathogen.

vitalism Ancient theory that living things had a force that gave them life. Nonliving things were thought not to have this force.

Biology Editorial Office
MDPI
Postfach, CH-4005
Basel, Switzerland
Web site: http://www.mdpi.com/journal
/biology
Biology is an international, peer-
reviewed, open access journal of
biological science, published by
MDPI online quarterly.

The Biology Project
Dept. of Biochemistry and Molecular
Biophysics
College of Science
The University of Arizona
P.O. Box 210041
1306 East University Boulevard
Tucson, AZ 85721-0041
(520) 621-6354
Web site: http://www.biology.arizona.edu/
The Biology Project delivers student-
oriented, highly interactive biology-
centered learning materials online.
These learning materials are used to
support biology lecture, laboratory,
and discussion sessions of general
education courses. The Biology
Project is fun, richly illustrated, and
tested on thousands of students. It
has been designed for biology students specifically who will benefit
from the real-life applications of biology and the inclusion of up-to-date
research findings.

Brookhaven National Lab
Biosciences Department
P.O. Box 5000

Upton, NY 11973-5000
(631) 344-8000
Web site: http://www.bnl.gov
/biosciences/
The Biosciences Department of
Brookhaven National Lab is focused
on synthetic biology, radiobiology,
computational biology, and structural biology and the
characterization of biological systems. The department is home to
Radiotracer Chemistry,
Instrumentation, and Biological
Imaging (RCIBI), a suite of tools
available for researching plant
metabolism, drug development, and
neuroimaging. Together with the
Collider-Accelerator Department,
Biosciences operates the NASA
Space Radiation Laboratory (NSRL),
used by radiobiologists and physi-
cists to study space radiation effects.

Centers for Disease Control and
Prevention (CDC)
1600 Clifton Road
Atlanta, GA 30333
800-CDC-INFO (232-4636)
Web site: http://www.cdc.gov
The CDC's mission is to create the
expertise, information, and tools that
people and communities need to
protect their health through health
promotion; prevention of disease,
injury and disability; and prepared-
ness for new health threats.
The CDC seeks to accomplish its mission by working with partners
throughout the nation and the world

to monitor health, detect and investigate health problems, conduct research to enhance prevention, develop and advocate sound public health policies, implement prevention strategies, promote healthy behaviors, foster safe and healthful environments, and provide leadership and training.

Khan Academy
P.O. Box 1630
Mountain View, CA 94042
Web site: http://www.khanacademy.org
/science/biology
Khan Academy is a not-for-profit educational organization whose mission is to provide a free, world-class education to anyone, anywhere. It has an entire section devoted to biology, including evolution and natural selection, cells and cell division, heredity and genetics, cellular respiration, the tree of life, photosynthesis, human biology, and immunology. Its other online materials cover subjects ranging from math and finance to history and art. With thousands of bite-sized videos, step-by-step problems, and instant data, Khan Academy provides a rich and engaging learning experience.

The National Science Foundation Directorate for Biological Sciences
4201 Wilson Boulevard
Arlington, VA 22230
(703) 292-5111
Web site: http://www.nsf.gov/dir
/index.jsp?org=BIO
The mission of the Directorate for Biological Sciences (BIO) is to enable discoveries for understanding life. BIO-supported research advances the frontiers of biological knowledge, increases our understanding of complex systems, and provides a theoretical basis for original research in many other scientific disciplines. The Directorate for Biological Sciences supports research to advance understanding of the principles and mechanisms governing life. Research studies extend across systems that encompass biological molecules, cells, tissues, organs, organisms, populations, communities, and ecosystems up to and including the global biosphere. NSF/BIO plays a major role in support of research resources for the biological sciences including living stock centers, systematics collections, biological field stations, computerized databases including sequence databases for plants and microorganisms. NSF/BIO is also the nation's principal supporter of fundamental academic research on plant biology, environmental biology, and biodiversity.

PLOS Biology
1160 Battery Street
Koshland Building East, Suite 100
San Francisco, CA 94111
(415) 624-1200
Web site: http://www.plosbiology.org

PLOS Biology is an open-access, peer-reviewed general biology journal published by PLOS, a nonprofit organization of scientists and physicians committed to making the world's scientific and medical literature a public resource. New articles are published online weekly; issues are published monthly.

Popular Science
2 Park Avenue, 9th Floor
New York, NY 10016
Web site: http://www.popsci.com
/category/tags/biology
Popular Science has been a leading source of science and technology news since its inception in 1872. PopSci.com first came online in 1999 and ever since has been renowned for its exciting and comprehensive daily content, including up-to-the-minute tech news, insightful commentary on the newest innovations, and scientific takes on what's new and what's next.

WEB SITES

Due to the changing nature of Internet links, Rosen Publishing has developed an online list of Web sites related to the subject of this book. This site is updated regularly. Please use this link to access this list:

http://www.rosenlinks.com/CORE/Bio

Alberts, Bruce, et al. *Essential Cell Biology*. New York, NY: Garland Science, 2009.

Distefano, Matthew. *Homework Helpers: Biology*. Pompton Plains, NJ: Career Press, 2011.

Freeman, Scott. *Biological Science*. New York, NY: Benjamin Cummings, 2008.

Hoefnagels, Mariëlle. *Biology: The Essentials*. New York, NY: McGraw-Hill Science/Engineering/Math, 2012.

Kratz, René Fester, and Donna Rae Siegfried. *Biology for Dummies*. Hobooken, NJ: For Dummies, 2010.

Krogh, David. *Biology: A Guide to the Natural World*. New York, NY: Benjamin Cummings, 2010.

Mader, Sylvia. *The Concepts of Biology*. New York, NY: McGraw-Hill Science/Engineering/Math, 2010.

Mader, Sylvia. *Lab Manual for Biology*. New York, NY: McGraw-Hill Science/Engineering/Math, 2012.

Mader, Sylvia, and Michael Windelspecht. *Biology*. New York, NY: McGraw-Hill Science/Engineering/Math, 2012.

Mader, Sylvia, and Michael Windelspecht. *Human Biology*. New York, NY: McGraw-Hill Science/Engineering/Math, 2011.

Reece, Jane B., et al. *Campbell Biology*. Ninth Edition. New York, NY: Benjamin Cummings, 2010.

Reece, Jane B., et al. *Study Guide for Campbell Biology*. New York, NY: Benjamin Cummings, 2010.

Russell, Peter J. *Biology: The Dynamic Science*. Independence, KY: Brooks Cole, 2011.

Shuster, Michele. *Scientific American Biology for a Changing World*. New York, NY: W. H. Freeman, 2011.

Starr, Cecie. *Biology: The Unity and Diversity of Life*. Independence, KY: Brooks Cole, 2008.

PHOTO CREDITS

Cover, p. 3 Visuals Unlimited, Inc./Victor Habbick/Getty Images; p. 6 Mark Conlin/ Oxford Scientific/Getty Images; p. 8 Richard Griffin/Shutterstock.com; p. 9 Cultura Science/Rolf Ritter/Oxford Scientific/Getty Images; p. 10 (top) John Carey/ Photolibrary/Getty Images; p. 11 Martin Shields/Photo Researchers/Getty Images; p. 14 Karel Gallas/Shutterstock.com; p. 15 Education Images/Universal Images Group/ Getty Images; p. 19 (left) Stefan Petru Andronache/Shutterstock.com; p. 19 (right) outdoorsman/Shutterstock.com; p. 20 Straublund Photography/Flickr/Getty Images; p. 25 Isabelle Plasschaert/Photolibrary/Getty Images; pp. 26, 46 iStockphoto/Thinkstock; p. 27 Mint Images-Frans Lanting/Getty Images; p. 28 MedicalRF.com/Getty Images; p. 29 Hoberman Collection/Universal Images Group/Getty Images; p. 39 (bottom) David M. Phillips/Science Source; p. 40 James Gerholdt/Peter Arnold/Getty Images; p. 42 © Jim West/PhotoEdit; p. 44 U.S. Geological Survey, Upper Midwest Environmental Sciences Center; p. 49 hraska/Shutterstock.com; p. 52 Sean Justice/Taxi/Getty Images; p. 53 P.E. Reed/The Image Bank/Getty Images; p. 55 Trevor Lush/The Image Bank/Getty Images; p. 56 G. Tompkinson/Science Source; p. 58 Photo Researchers/Getty Images; p. 59 Stephen Simpson/Taxi/Getty Images; pp. 60, 61, 62 © AP Images; p. 66 Thomas Kokta/Peter Arnold/Getty Images; p. 67 Emil Von Maltitz/Oxford Scientific/Getty Images; p. 68 (top) Science Source/Getty Images; p. 69 The Bridgeman Art Library/ Getty Images; p. 70 Mark Gibson/Visuals Unlimited/Getty Images; p. 71 Marevision/age fotostock/Getty Images; p. 72 Andrew Syred/Science Source; p. 73 Scott Camazine/Photo Researchers/Getty Images; p. 74 Alfred Eisenstaedt/Time & Life Pictures/Getty Images; p. 75 Popperfoto/Getty Images; p. 77 Science Source; p. 79 Universal Images Group/Getty Images; p. 81 Fritz Goro/Time & Life Pictures/Getty Images; interior pages background images © iStockphoto.com/Sebastian Kaulitzki (borders), © iStockphoto.com/Sergey Yeremin; top of pp. 6, 17, 32, 42, 52, 62, 66, 74 © iStockphoto.com/aleksandar velasevic; all other photos and illustrations © Brown Bear Books Ltd.